"Marketing Unmasked is a very rare book. It gives the small business owner everything they need to know to be a successful brand. Everything. Not only have Wolf and Frost covered every imaginable angle brilliantly, they have done it in a style that makes the ideas and actions easy to adopt. Well done."

**Sharon Drew Morgen: author of <u>Dirty Little Secrets:</u>
<u>why buyers can't buy and sellers can't sell</u>
<u>and what you can do about it</u>**

"Lots of books on branding will tell you the strategy but don't share the tactics because they want you to come to them for the answers. Erik and Stephanie believe differently. They want you to come to them for creative implementations (no book can teach you that) because they've already given you the answers in their book. If you're a small business looking to move from having a logo to building a brand, this book belongs with you and your team. The information you need to know is probably already in the order you're asking questions."

**Mike Wittenstein: "The Authority on Customer Experience"
Speaker, Consultant, Chief Experience Officer at Storyminers**

"Wolf & Frost have given us a rare gift in Marketing Unmasked — an easy read for attacking the hard problems. 'Unmasked' cuts through all the academic babble and misdirection like a fine blade crafting a choice cut. We're spared the 'fat' and served only the prime meat — the knowledge, tools and insight we need to go to market, and the confidence of knowing what to do when we get there."

**Stone Payton: Author, Speaker,
Host of High Velocity Radio**

marketing: unmasked

insider's tips + tricks for success
in small business marketing

by erik wolf + stephanie frost
edited by emily capps

zodo group | atlanta, ga

Portions of this book first appeared on the authors' website.

Marketing: Unmasked
By Erik Wolf and Stephanie Frost
Edited by Emily Capps
Design and graphics by Erik Wolf, Alexandra Nathan and Keith Fletcher
Typeset by Alexandra Nathan

ISBN 978-0-615-32550-7

Printed in the United States of America

ACKNOWLEDGMENTS

We are very grateful to the many people who helped us with this book, but none more than our editor Emily Capps who put in countless hours reading and rereading this book. Without her, we can honestly say that Marketing: Unmasked would never gotten done.

We would also like to thank Alexandra Nathan and Keith Fletcher who contributed tremendously to the look and layout of this book.

Thank you also to Lee Kantor, who invites us into the RadioX studio every Tuesday and does an oustanding job producing our show *Gravity Free Radio*. The show has been an incredible resource for us in our writing. Thanks as well to all of our wonderful guests who have been an inspiration.

And we certainly can't forget our family, friends and colleagues who have encouraged us along the way. We appreciate everything you have done for us.

TABLE OF CONTENTS

"Remarkable marketing is the art of building things worth noticing."

- SETH GODIN

I was doing a crossword puzzle the other day and the clue for 11 Down — a four-letter word — was "marketed." The answer? "Sold."

If only it were that easy. Wouldn't it be wonderful if the act of offering a product up to the marketplace were enough to get results? Unfortunately though, marketing is rarely that simple. For many small business owners, marketing can be frustrating and downright confounding. The direct mail piece you thought was a sure thing did nothing, yet that talk you gave at the Chamber of Commerce got you three promising leads. Why?

Stephanie and I wrote this book to help small business owners effectively navigate the strange — and sometimes confusing — marketing landscape. And, as both a small business marketer and a small business owner, I know about that struggle.

Although not intentionally, I've been writing this book since I first left my job as a corporate marketing director to work full-time with small businesses in 2006. I have been through all of the struggles mentioned above both with my clients and with my own business. Ultimately, I've lived the ups and downs on both sides. Even with many years of marketing experience and exposure to a variety of things in my corporate career, the rules change when you're an entrepreneur.

For me, the big awakening was no longer having a clear definition in my job. I didn't get to just sit in my office anymore and come up with creative ideas — I also had to execute them from start to finish, justify them financially and plan for any expenses, source and qualify external resources, negotiate the contracts, and be my own salesman. Oh, and by the way, selling is not easy.

There's a lot that many of us take for granted working in a corporate environment. If an invoice comes in, all you need to do is jot your initials and someone in accounting "automagically" takes care of it. You don't even need to worry about walking over to deliver that invoice to accounting because your inter-office mail will handle that. As a marketer, I took our company's experienced sales force for granted. And my team and me? We were similarly underappreciated.

But entrepreneurship is a great equalizer. We all have to do a little bit of everything and so we can finally understand what our coworkers were trying to explain to us all those years.

I also never realized — until I had to do it all for myself — how different marketing at the small business level really was. In many fields, operating at this level is a lot like the enterprise level, only smaller. Good accounting practices are good accounting practices, no matter how big your business is.

But I quickly learned that marketing strategy at the small business level runs almost completely opposite to big business practices. Big businesses love advertising, which is often a bad idea for entrepreneurs. Big businesses have both large internal marketing staffs and big agencies at their disposal to execute; entrepreneurs have, well... themselves. Big businesses can afford risky behavior and are prepared for some inevitable failures along the way. By contrast, small businesses tend to shy away from risk and sometimes feel pressured either by time or budget to "put all their eggs in one basket" and lay their hopes on a single initiative.

"You're going to fail more often than you succeed as a business person, and you can't be afraid of that. You have to be willing to take risks," says Todd Schnick, an Atlanta-based marketing expert. "Think through strategically what your goals are and what your messaging is and once you're there, you can take more aggressive risks on trying different things. When you fail, you're going to learn things that you can apply and move forward from there."

• • •

This is not intended to be a small business marketing "bible" and it's not necessarily a "how to." We don't expect that anyone will be able to flip through this book and suddenly become a marketing genius overnight.

Stephanie and I hope that the information and examples in this book will help you make better and more informed decisions about your marketing and that it will help you organize your thoughts about marketing strategically. We have also included a lot of helpful hints along the way, giving you the inside perspective on what works for small businesses, what doesn't work and what is a waste of time — or worse — a rip off. We wanted to "take off the mask" and provide open, honest advice — a rare commodity for a lot of entrepreneurs who are used to conflicting information provided mostly by people looking to sell you their services.

It's hard to find success in that kind of environment and even harder to maintain focus on the task at hand.

Hopefully our book will give you some insight. We've organized Marketing Unmasked like a tapas menu, giving you little tastes of many different flavors like branding, logo design, marketing planning, web design, and social media — one of the newest and most mystifying ingredients in a small business marketing strategy.

Hopefully we'll give you enough information to understand how you should be using these tools to your advantage and then put you on the path towards integrating them into your plan. There's even information here on hiring a good marketing, branding, or design partner. We've also included some do-it-yourself tips throughout, but there are already a lot of good books that can give you a detailed look at one or more of the topics we've covered here.

There's a marketing monster waiting to be unleashed inside the depths of your small business and we hope that this book helps you set it free.

-Erik Wolf, August 2009

Chapter 1

Building the small business brand

Of all the marketing challenges that a small business owner is likely to face, branding is one of the most esoteric, intangible, and generally difficult-to-grasp concepts.

It's hard to say exactly why this happens. However, in our experience working with entrepreneurs, it seems that objectivity and perspective are central to the issue.

Being a small business owner means that you — by definition — cannot be counted on to be objective in your views, your perspective, or your decisions. Entrepreneurs are dreamers and visionaries; people who single-mindedly (and oftentimes single-handedly) work tirelessly on their enterprise. You are about as objective when it comes to your business as you are about your children, your spouse, or your favorite sports team — which is to say *not at all.*

As a consequence of living our businesses day and night, all too often we tell our company's story from our own point of view. We focus on the features of our product and service that we personally find most interesting or that were the most difficult to execute rather on what is most meaningful to our audience. We focus on "what our business does" rather than "what our business does *for you.*"

Look at the truly great brands: Apple, Starbucks, Nike, Mercedes. They are built around inspirational experiences and the aspirations of their customers, NOT on what they are selling on the surface. After all, there are a lot of companies out there that sell sneakers. Nike sells determination and a winning spirit. There are a lot of companies that sell computers, but none come with the combination of design, simplicity, and creativity that Apple does.

So what did Apple do that you can't? Absolutely nothing. Of course, this is an oversimplification, but all they really did was start with a basic idea about what Apple would be and then applied it consistently to every aspect of their organization.

In this chapter, we are going to walk you through what makes a small business brand — from the "fluffy" intangible stuff to picking a great name.

What is a "brand" anyway?
And how do I get one?

This is one of the most misunderstood words in the entire business lexicon. Some people believe that "branding" consists of the design and adoption of a logo. This is wrong.

Others believe that "branding" is the crafting and adoption of a name. This also is wrong.

Simply put, "branding" is the crafting and adoption of an experience. When we talk about a "brand" we're talking about the entire interaction that someone has with your business. It includes not only the graphics they see, but also the words they read, the words they hear and the emotions they feel. It includes every point of contact between you and your customer. Your logo, your website, your business card, your receptionist, your brochure, your order form, your sales team, and your product or service are all components of your brand.

You are your company's brain, but your brand is the soul — the intangible essence behind everything that your customers experience when they deal with your business.

If you think this sounds intangible, if you think it sounds like an initiative that will be difficult to tie back to a measurable ROI, you would be right. If you think branding sounds expensive — well, you may also be right. An agency would typically charge somewhere between $20K and $250K to help a company develop a brand strategy depending on the size of the firms involved and the scope of work.

But here are a few tips and secrets that will help you get the results you want without parting with what may be — especially for a new or very small business — a year's worth of profits:

1. Even though it may be almost impossible to quantify in a meaningful way, your branding initiative can't be wildly unprofitable. Keep your spending conservative. If you find a good consultant or firm that specializes in working with small businesses on small budgets, you may be surprised at what you can achieve for $3-5K.

2. Find someone with whom you can connect and speak openly. If you find yourself talking with a consultant who acts like they're better than you or makes you uncomfortable in any way, do NOT hire them. Their experience or track record doesn't matter at this point. There are plenty of brilliant people in this world that are terribly difficult to work with and the marketing industry seems to have more prima donnas per capita than most.

3. Come to the table with a list of documented, specific overall business goals if you do not have a written business plan. Your branding and marketing initiatives should

serve your vision for the business as a whole. Make sure you've got someone who is there to work on YOUR business and not reshape it in their own image.

4. As you'll see from reading this chapter, the biggest secret of all may be that hiring an expert to help you craft your brand isn't exactly like hiring a doctor to do that bypass surgery you need. If you can find the right person to work with — and if you can comfortably afford that kind of luxury — YES, hire a branding expert. Otherwise, there's plenty that can be done on your own — provided that you have a good chunk of time to devote and you don't have a problem connecting with the softer side of your business. There is plenty of info and free advice in this chapter to help you do just that. If you want to dive deeper, there are lots of other good books that can help.

INSIDER'S TIP: To keep the branding process grounded, we've often found that it helps to express your brand in terms of real things. It can often help to think of a brand as having qualities similar to a person. It's only natural to describe Nike in terms of people like Michael Jordan and Derek Jeter and so it may be similarly easy to put the qualities of your brand in terms of qualities you might associate with a celebrity or someone you know. We've also done exercises with business owners where we've looked at pictures of various animals, styles of homes, or foods to try to get at the essence of a brand. For example, dogs are loyal, reliable, and intelligent; squirrels are thrifty, quick, and adaptable. Panthers are wild, explosive, and athletic. Don't feel pressure to pull this stuff out of thin air, it may help to look at the world around you for inspiration.

So where do I start?

First thing's first. You can't see until you open your eyes.

Over time, industries tend to become a little like gated communities. People become focused on what their neighbors are doing and tend not to care what's happening in other neighborhoods. How often have you looked at one of your competitors and thought,

"They are offering a free trial. Maybe we should too."

Or, "They have a new packaged deal, we should do one like that."

Or, "They're offering their entry-level service at a new low price, should we follow?"

No one told you to seek out your competitors and borrow their business strategies but a lot of small business owners feel compelled nonetheless. We call this type of self-inflicted peer pressure "parroting." One competitor takes an action and, out of instinct, another repeats. And then another and another and another until everyone starts saying the exact same thing. A little later, someone will start saying something slightly different, but it never takes long for the rest of the parrots to catch on. So as long as we focus our attention exclusively on our own industry, it becomes very difficult for anyone to differentiate in any meaningful way.

And remember: Just because your competition is doing something, it doesn't mean it's successful. Unlike public companies, small businesses don't have regular SEC filings and financial press releases. We can't just open up their balance sheets and income statements and see how they're doing. Don't assume that all of your competition's new products/services are doing well just because they sound good on the website. "Me too" can be a disastrous strategy for a small business. But unfortunately, it's very easy to get sucked into.

The easiest way to get yourself out of the vicious cycle of "parroting" is to take off your blinders and start looking outside your industry for inspiration. Look at things that have nothing to do with your business. Go to the mall, browse on the Internet, learn about companies and industries you've never encountered. That's what will really inspire you and help you take your business to the next level.

In <u>Blue Ocean Strategy</u>, one of our favorite business books of all time, W. Chan Kim and Renée Mauborgne demonstrate that most companies within an industry compete based on a common set of factors. If you were a winemaker, key factors for competition are price, the prestige of your vineyard, and the complexity of the taste of your wines. Kim and Mauborgne suggest that true differentiation — and a profitable "Blue Ocean" — emerges when a competitor markets based on a new set of factors. When [yellow tail] created their wine, as one of the featured Blue Ocean Strategy cases goes, they eliminated the emphasis on complexity of taste and didn't address the history and heritage of their vineyard. Instead, they created a wine that was fun and easy-drinking for novices. Ideas that flew directly in the face of traditional wine marketing. The result? [yellow tail] captured a completely new group of wine drinkers and ultimately became the best-selling wine in the U.S.

It's definitely important to keep tabs on what's happening in your industry — we recommend doing a simple SWOT analysis (Strengths, Weaknesses, Opportunities, and Threats) and updating it two to four times a year. But once you understand your competition and how they compete, look to other industries for ideas. Taking off the blinders and studying a variety of businesses is an easy and surprisingly effective first step towards creating a brand unlike any others in your industry.

INSIDER'S TIP: Build a brain trust. As we've already discussed, you're too close to your business to see it from any perspective other than your own. Find a group of people who you can speak openly with about your business and, in particular, your marketing efforts. Who should be in your brain trust? Someone with marketing or branding experience would be a good start. If you don't know anyone who might be a good candidate to serve as your voice of reason from a marketing perspective, consider hiring one. Other strong additions would be business partners, a customer (or someone who fits the profile of a customer), a trusted vendor or strategic ally and just about anyone who will be honest with you and has good business sense. But remember, even though you should let people advise you, the end decision is yours. Your business isn't a democracy and you are under no obligation to treat it like one.

Know your customer

Who are your customers, really? And "mid-sized technology firms in the greater Atlanta metro area" is not an acceptable answer. Neither are "small business owners looking to expand through venture capital" or "college seniors." When you make a sale, it isn't to a business or to a group, it's always to an individual. Even if the check comes from a business account, it's still a single person that shook your hand, signed your contract and authorized the payment.

Now obviously, all people are different, but there are many commonalities that connect individuals who buy similar goods or services. For example, your customers may be predominantly male or female. Are they likely to be college educated? How old are they? How much money do they make? What kind of car do they drive? Suddenly your generic, faceless demographic profile starts to look like a real person.

Erik worked for a baby toy manufacturer for several years and even in that environment, marketing to a very narrow demographic (pregnant women and moms with children less than 18 months old) his executive team STILL didn't completely understand who their audience was. How is that possible? Well, it's easy. The company had grown up — pardon the pun — in the early 1990s and they had made a name for themselves marketing infant toys and products in black, white, and red. The high-contrast color scheme was designed to appeal to babies — who have very limited vision as newborns — and stimulate early development.

The products sparked a major trend in the industry: "educational" toys for babies. Because of that early success, company executives had always believed that "learning" was a major component to success in the marketplace and that it was very important to moms. In 2001, it appeared that the line was running out of gas, so management decided it was time to retool their brand and — on the advice of an outside marketing group — settled on a platform built around "learning together" with mom and baby. It didn't work. In 2004, the project came to Erik and he had to figure out why they had failed. He soon found his answer.

It turns out that in 2004 the average age of new moms was 27, which meant that most of these women were in middle school when company executives were deciding what would be important to them as new moms. These women were different than the women that bought the black, white, and red toys ten years earlier. In the early '90s, most new moms were Baby Boomers or very early Generation X'ers. In 2004, the majority of new moms were Generation X and a sizable amount of Generation Y. A great many of them came from divorced families. They also grew up with computers and with ubiquitous advertising. Research also showed that while only about a third of Baby Boomer moms stayed home with the kids, about half of our new moms did. They had different experiences and different priorities.

And, where the baby boomer moms wanted smart babies, the moms of 2004 wanted happy babies. It was a major shift and a big eye-opener. But to really build a brand around new moms, Erik and his team took the exercise one step further.

Starting with a basic 27-year-old new mom that stays at home — at the time the company did its research about half of new moms were staying home, a major increase over baby boomer moms — Erik and his team fabricated the rest of the specifics of her life based on trends and research. She and her husband owned a mid-sized suburban home. She drove a modestly priced "crossover" SUV. She liked to eat healthy and exercise and stayed very busy running the household. When shopping, she looked for value over brand names and was skeptical when it came to lofty promises in advertising. She spent much of her free time online. They documented what magazines she would read, what websites she would visit, what stores she would shop in. They even gave her a name. It was Jennifer, a very common name for women who were born in the mid-to-late 1970's.

Erik's team spent a lot of time creating and refining the "Jennifer" profile, but it was worth the effort. When they were done, they knew her so well it was almost like having a real mom on the branding team. Whenever they came to a point in the process where a decision had to be made, Jennifer became a sort of litmus test. "Would this be something Jennifer would buy?"

And because they looked at her as if she was real person, she was key in helping the team overcome that curse of knowledge we discussed earlier. Especially when it came to specific messages. Were specific words and phrases being included because they were important to the team or because they would be important to Jennifer? The superficial messages didn't make the cut, but the meaningful ones did.

Putting together a customer profile will take some time — especially if you go as in depth as Erik's group did, but it will pay huge dividends as your brand starts to take shape. We've done this exercise with clients many times and it has always been worthwhile.

Is your customer base too diverse to be summed up by one person? Do as many as you need. But make sure that every customer profile you build is critical to developing a successful brand.

In Erik's example, the team considered developing a grandparent/gift-giver profile as well, but that customer wasn't nearly as important and in many cases may not have even been a decision maker in the baby toy aisle. Many grandparents consult with their sons/daughters about baby gifts before purchase. The popularity of baby registries — which also allow parents-to-be to suggest specific products as gifts — also made it difficult to clearly identify the gift-giver as a distinct customer. At the end of the day, it really seemed like Jennifer was making the majority of decisions.

But if you do truly sell to two different types of people, say a business audience and a government audience or a male audience and a female audience (like a clothing company for example) it would be very beneficial to create multiple customer profiles.

When you're done, these customers will be among your most prized assets as a business owner. Erik had his design team make a big collage about Jennifer and mount it on a foamcore board. They had pictures of her favorite products, the logos of her favorite stores, and a set of photos discovered on a stock photography site became her family pictures. Erik kept it in his office and even brought the Jennifer board to a few meetings to help demonstrate the rationale behind some of their branding decisions. She made it to several sales calls with key accounts as well.

There are few things in marketing more important than being comfortable with the group of people you are marketing to.

What's important to your brand? (The Words)

Or a better way to ask it would be, what's important to you as a business owner? What's truly important about the way you deliver your product or service? What do you want your customers to remember? Some people say, "Integrity."

Others may say "Creativity," "Innovation," "Organic," or "Service."

Marketers have all kinds of fancy terms for these words — they might call them "core attributes," "core values," or "brand essence." Regardless of what you call them though, these words are going to be the foundation of your brand. So for simplicity, we'll just call them "The Words." They will drive everything from here on.

The Words are a tough concept to "get." So here is how we explain it: Think about someone you know really well. Maybe your husband or wife, your father or best friend. What words would you associate with that person? Nouns and adjectives are both acceptable. You might look at your best friend and say, "She's 'honest,' 'hardworking,' and always 'does what she says.'" Those are her Words.

The Words obviously can't describe everything about this person — her history, hobbies, career goals, or hair color — but it does create a baseline that "grounds" your perception of her and helps explain other elements of her persona and the experience you've had with her as a friend. But most importantly, without these values she'd be an entirely different person.

What are the elements of your brand that you want to be most memorable? What elements of your vision as a business owner do you want to translate directly to your customers' experience in dealing with your company? What elements are so central to your service that you couldn't afford to lose them? Is it quality? Customer service? A commitment to philanthropy? There are no right or wrong answers as long as you truly believe in them.

Some businesses are truly built around their owners. Think of Richard Branson of Virgin or Donald Trump. In this case, The Words for the brand and the owner are one and the same. If your business is built around you and your personal vision, think about what your values are and jot them down. Or have someone who knows you well help you.

In United We Brand, Mike Moser suggests a slightly more morbid exercise to help business owners figure out what their company's Words are. He calls it "The Tombstone Exercise." If your company were to go out of business today, what would go on your tombstone? What would your customers miss most about you? If one of your customers delivered your eulogy, what would they say?

Try it with some brands you know:

Google: "I'll miss their innovative approach to the web."

IKEA: "I'll miss their style and affordability."

Caribou Coffee: "I'll miss the comfortable atmosphere and the taste of their coffee."

These are all elements that are definitely central to these brands — and if you were to ask several people you would probably get similar answers. Obviously, no one wants to be in the position of eulogizing their own company, but it is an effective way to get at the information you need.

Differentiate!

Jamie Turner, author of the prominent marketing blog *The 60 Second Marketer* says, "For a small- to mid-size business person, one of the first things you want to do is get back to figuring out what it is that really differentiates you from your competitors and make sure it comes out in everything you do."

This is a very big topic and, frankly, it seems a little cheap on our part to devote only a section of a chapter to such a supremely important subject. When you're done with this appetizer though, if you want to learn more, check out Seth Godin's classic, The Purple Cow.

It's impossible to talk about branding without discussing differentiation. After all, how can you communicate the value of something without discussing its relative uniqueness in the marketplace?

We encourage all of our clients to spend some serious time thinking about differentiation and what their unique value proposition is. Then we encourage them to write it down because it's just that important. Unfortunately though, "differentiation" has become one of those vague, overused marketing words and not many people know what it really means anymore or how you know if you've achieved it.

We have a simple four-step test we use to help our clients determine if they have truly hit on a valuable point of differentiation. If you have successfully come up with some Words for your brand after reading the last section, you should be in good shape to figure out if they will help you succeed in the marketplace:

1. **Is it unique?** If you're offering the same product or service as everyone else, why should anyone buy yours? There needs to be SOMETHING that makes yours unique.

2. **Is it meaningful?** If you've passed the first step, congratulations — you are different. But why should anyone care? Consider your Words from the last section and the Tombstone Exercise. If your point of differentiation — no matter how unique — isn't worth talking about, you need to toss it out and start again.

3. **Does it create value?** By being the company that you've described using your Words, can you save your clients time or money? Or, can you help them sell more? If you aren't hitting at least one of these three, start over.

4. Is it sustainable? If others in your industry can easily imitate your value proposition, it can't be a true differentiator. Great points of differentiation will be difficult or nearly impossible to knock off.

One last important point about one of the MOST differentiating factors for any small business: It's the reason that your clients should buy from YOU and not your competition. And it isn't your pricing, it isn't your assortment of products and / or services, your infrastructure, your website, or the terms of your contract.

Those things are all important but when searching for true differentiation, most entrepreneurs really just need to look in the mirror. It's YOUR vision that makes your company unique, YOUR background, YOUR body of work, YOUR ability to care for a client. The most significant ingredient in your unique value proposition is YOU.

Don't be afraid to leverage yourself in your sales and marketing efforts. Small businesses can't afford to be faceless, impersonal entities like Fortune 500 companies. Take credit for the pieces of you that have been invested in your business. It's the one thing that your competitors really can't replicate.

CONTROVERSIAL TOPIC: Everyone has a different approach to crafting a meaningful differentiation strategy. There are some schools of thought that would suggest that just about anything that will help you stand apart from the crowd is a good thing. In our opinion — and in our experience — being different isn't a high enough standard; we believe differentiation is useless unless it helps you sell your product or service. Regardless of how you choose to approach this in your own business, make sure that you're comfortable with the direction that you choose. Don't allow yourself to be talked into something you don't believe in, no matter how wildly creative it is. If you don't believe in what you're selling, it will shine through and compromise your efforts.

Write a Positioning Statement

Once you have some Words and an understanding of what makes you unique, a positioning statement is a great way to put those tools to use. Positioning statements are short one-to-two sentence strategy summaries that broadly define who your company is, who you sell to, and how you differentiate from your competition. There are many formats for writing a positioning statement, but below is the one we've come to like best. It works like "Mad Libs" — just fill in the blanks:

To/For [a target audience] **who** [qualifier or need], [your company/brand] **is a** [describe industry/ category] **that** [value proposition]. **And unlike** [competition], [point of differentiation].

As an example, here's one that we wrote for our business Zero-G Creative:

For small business owners and entrepreneurs **who** need high-end marketing, web and graphics expertise to help grow their small enterprise, Zero-G Creative **is a** new kind of agency **that** is specifically designed to meet the needs and budgets of small businesses and startups. **And unlike other** agencies, design boutiques, and freelancers, Zero-G Creative can make high-end consulting and design available to small clients at affordable prices.

That says simply and concisely what our brand is, the group of people we're targeting and what sets us apart from the competition. It can also help answer questions about what we should consider as new service offerings or brand extensions and what we should invest in.

For example, if we were offered an opportunity to engage in a strategic partnership with a firm that sold goods or services complimentary to ours, we'd want to ask ourselves a series of questions to make sure that it meshed with our strategy:

1. Does this benefit small business owners?
2. Does it help us deliver high-quality marketing, graphic, or web design services?
3. Can it be delivered "affordably" on a small budget?
4. Does it help us maintain high standards of quality and customer service?

If the answers to these questions are "yes" then the service will probably make a good addition to our portfolio. If we answered "no" to any, we should probably re-evaluate. In doing this kind of litmus test, we also consider indifferent answers (i.e., partnering with a high-end video studio doesn't hurt our chances of delivering high quality marketing, web, or design services) to be "no's."

Whether you're talking about a new product or service, a new vendor, partnership, or even an accounting or CRM system, if it won't HELP you deliver on the promise of your brand it probably isn't worth your time.

INSIDER'S TIP: While a positioning statement isn't exactly an elevator speech, go ahead and commit yours to memory. Oftentimes business owners stumble when they are asked what makes their company different. Try asking that question to a few entrepreneurs this week and see what happens.

Some will turn red and suddenly develop a case of modesty. Some will dive inside their own head and talk about some obscure innovation or feature that is much more exciting to them personally than it ever will be to a real customer. Some will just plain trip over their words. Only one or two out of every ten people we ask this question to can provide a concise and coherent answer to what should be a very easy question. Never turn down an opportunity to help someone understand what makes you different —whether you think they will ever do business with you or not.

So what's in a name?

If you've got a name for your business and you love it, great. Skip this section and pat yourself on the back for successfully accomplishing something very difficult. If not, read on.

Naming isn't easy. But hopefully by now you've caught on to why our spiel about naming comes at the end of the branding chapter and not the beginning.

Yes, you've guessed it: we've made a very difficult job a little bit easier by creating some standards that will help you objectively evaluate the myriad of name suggestions you are likely to compile. If your name does not reflect the spirit of your Words and positioning statement, discard it. If you don't believe it will appeal to your target audience, discard it.

For example, if your business concept is all about hands-on customer service, you might not want to name your business Soloko or something that insinuates that the customer is on their own. If you're an interior designer serving a high-end clientele, we would similarly recommend against calling your business Rottweiler Interiors, no matter how much you love your dog.

So how do you find a name that works for your business?

There are some easy tips and tricks that we'll get into in just a minute but first, some simple guidelines that we try to adhere to when we help a client name their business:

1. **Keep it short:** Long names are difficult to remember and are often destined to be shortened into acronyms or nicknames by everyone who does business with you. Some nicknames can be unfortunate. Let's leave it at that.

2. **Unique:** Stay away from names that sound similar to your competitors. Some people might think it's a little fun, a little "cheeky" to pick a name that has a familiar ring to it within the industry but all this will cause is confusion. Also stay away also from cliché and commodity words like "solutions," "first," and "digital." And with everyone trying to cash in on the environment these days, we'd also include words like "green," "eco," and "Earth," on that list. These words don't add anything to your name and are virtually meaningless. You might consider making a word up, using your name or a derivative of it or drawing inspiration from a foreign language.

3. **Easy to read:** Especially when you get into the realm of words that may have a foreign origin or may be completely made up, make sure that it is still easy to pronounce. It doesn't help you to have a name your customers and business partners are unable to read.

4. **Web-able:** You need to be able to get a good URL for your business. If you can't obtain a web address that works well with the name you're looking at, drop it. Your online presence is very important. Don't spend time pursuing a name that you can't use online.

5. **On brand:** It needs to fit with your strategy. This is mandatory. The attitude your name conveys must match what you've written about your brand. Everything that your customers come into contact with needs to present a cohesive statement.

And by all means, do some research! If you have the budget for a lawyer to do a full trademark search, that would be advisable. If you'd rather hold off on that, at least do a Google search and check the domain name at GoDaddy or another domain registration site (don't just type the domain name into your browser and assume that the name is available because nothing came up — do a proper domain search). These simple steps will save you a LOT of heartache down the line.

Case in point: We worked with a client who was marketing a line of environmentally-friendly cleaning products designed for commercial/industrial use. The name of their brand was very generic and loaded with typical environmental buzzwords. Problem? They did not check out the name before they did their logo, website, business cards, and packaging design. They found out after the fact that it was already in use by a firm who had a potential trademark conflict.

Another problem: They quickly fell in love with a new name (which also contained an eco buzzword) and discovered it was the name of a book.

You really need to check this stuff out and do the due diligence before committing to a name.

INSIDER'S TIP: It's not necessary to name your business after the product you make or the service you perform. We had a discussion recently with an entrepreneur who was off to a slow start in her naming process. "But how will anyone know what I do? " she asked. We don't believe that your business name alone needs to tell your whole story. We prefer business names that are derived from the intangibles: How you make your customers feel, what they are able to achieve by way of their relationship with you. If you're nervous about moving forward with a name that abstracts what you do, consider launching with a tagline that describes what you do concisely. And as your business inevitably evolves over time, taglines can be changed or removed a lot more easily than business names can.

The elusive "made up" name

With an increasingly crowded marketplace and the availability of decent .com domain names dwindling, the idea of making up a word to use as a business name is becoming very popular. So how exactly do you go about inventing a brand new, never-before-spoken word?

It's not always easy, but there are ways to help kick-start the process. Combining words or names can help and we also find that there is fantastic inspiration to be drawn from the animal kingdom and from foreign languages.

For example, we once did a naming project for an entrepreneur in the healthcare industry. His business helped primary care physicians negotiate more advantageous rates with the insurance providers and — in exchange for the improved rates — helped the insurance providers better manage their risk in dealing with the physicians. Essentially, his business existed where the interests of these two parties came together.

He really liked the word "vertex" to describe this meeting point. As a business name, however, Vertex was unavailable and we were afraid that it sounded too "high tech," a quality that would likely not be popular among his physician constituents.

So we started translating "vertex" into other languages and we stumbled upon something interesting: Vertex translated into the much softer, more elegant-sounding "vertice" in both Italian and Portuguese. The only problem was that it was difficult to pronounce. But once we rewrote it more phonetically as "vertisy" the business owner fell in love with it. It was short, simple, unique, and the ideal domain name "vertisy.com" was available.

Spelling, in particular is something that you can have a lot of fun with when you're doing this type of exercise. As long as the word remains easy to read, there are absolutely no rules. Use letters that improve the visual appearance of the word. Change ordinary and familiar words into something new and fun. As you're doing this kind of tweaking, it's especially helpful to brainstorm on a whiteboard or big piece of poster board. Everyone is different of course, but we've always found that being able to stare at our options helps us get a better feel for what's there and what we might be able to do to take our concept to the next level.

And, if you don't speak several languages fluently, you might also try an online translation tool like BabelFish (Google it if you haven't heard of it) to help you get going.

INSIDER'S TIP: Domain names are extremely important but unfortunately domain names ending in .com (and sometimes even .net and .org) can be hard to come by. Using a fictional word increases your odds of finding something available but even then there are no guarantees. So what do you do?

While it's always most intuitive to use the name of your company as your web address, you might also consider creating a phrase or tagline to use as a url. For example, as of this writing, "WeKnowBranding. com" was still available. If we were starting a new practice dedicated solely to branding, we might buy and use this url if the name of our company was for some reason unavailable.

There are also a lot of new domain extensions available like .me, .us, .nu and .ws. While it might not scream credibility to have your web address be your company name followed by .me, you can use these extensions to spell words and phrases. For example, if we were to open a Mexican restaurant called Hint of Lime, as of this writing we could secure the domain name "hintofli.me" even though hintoflime.com was already taken.

Chapter 2

Design for success: logos, colors + collateral

So what's so important about design anyway? Why does it matter how good my business looks in the marketplace?

That's the second most common question that small business owners ask us (the most common, by the way is "What's all this about social media?" but we're saving that for a later chapter).

Here's the short answer: Why do something halfway when it takes roughly the same amount of time, the same amount of effort and the same amount of money to do something right?

Now, here's the longer answer. People are pretty smart and they process information a whole lot faster than you'd think.

The first few seconds after you meet someone are often the most influential few seconds in an entire relationship. In less time than it would take to shake hands, you're already making split-second decisions about what you think of this person, how they're dressed, whether they look you in the eye, etc. It's part of human nature. Malcolm Gladwell wrote a whole book about it called Blink and it's a must-read.

We do the same thing in business. Whether we like it or not, our potential customers judge us by our "stuff" — logos, business cards, websites, brochures, etc.. If those important customer-facing tools look unpolished and unprofessional, so do we.

The flip side is that if we really make the effort to look good, we can turn those tools into a strategic advantage. A great business card WILL get compliments and great-looking websites can still impress people. You can make yourself look bigger and better than your competition.

No matter what the industry, well-designed businesses are just more appealing. Not convinced? What made the iPod the most popular MP3 player around? More storage? Longer battery life? Outstanding sound quality? No, it really isn't better than the other players on the market. It's just cooler. Other MP3 players just look cheap and inferior next to the iPod. And especially back when the iPod was new, there was some status to be had by being seen in public with those white earbuds.

It's the same reason that people pay two or three times more for stainless steel appliances and why, given the choice, many people we know would rather shop in Target than Wal-Mart. Looks matter. And if you think that logic doesn't extend to your business, you'd be kidding yourself.

But here's the good news: It really doesn't take anything extra to design your business for success. It takes the same about of time, money, and effort to get a good logo as a lousy one. If anything, it's cheaper to go for good design out of the gate because you won't want to replace it right away with something new. And it won't cost you sales or opportunities. So why not just do it right from the start?

In this chapter, we're going to walk through the ins and outs of small business design, including logos, business cards, and marketing collateral. And don't worry, we haven't forgotten about web design; we've devoted an entire chapter to that topic.

Do I need an icon in my logo or not?

There are a lot of great icons in the world — the Nike Swoosh, the Target bull's-eye, and Disney's Mickey Mouse Ears are among them. But a lot of us forget that some of the best and most recognizable logos in the world don't use icons at all. Think of Google, The Gap, ebay, IBM, and countless others.

But strangely, if you show a small business owner a clean, beautiful type-based logo for their business, they are unlikely to select it. We've talked to a lot of entrepreneurs about this and the main issue behind this phenomenon goes beyond what a business owner believes may actually be right or wrong for their business. It's a psychological block that says "What am I paying this designer for? All they did was type a word. I could have done that!" They feel that the designer has cheated them by not attempting to design an icon and that they took the easy way out.

From a design perspective, many designers will tell you that type-based logos are the most challenging to work on. Without an icon to hide behind, designers tend to obsess about the tiny, seemingly insignificant details a lot more and agonize over each and every letter. And further, if a designer has taken the time to create a type-based logo, it probably means that they think it has merit for their client's brand.

So why don't we give more consideration to the type-based logos? Don't let "I could have done that" stand in the way of doing the right thing for your brand. Anyone could cut a piece of uncooked fish and throw it down on a plate, but few of us would ever be mistaken for a sushi chef.

It's the same thing with graphic design. The simple ideas require just as much artistic vision as the complex ones and they require the same set of skills to execute properly. So please give the simple ideas a chance. And don't let the "I could have done that" instinct ruin a great idea for you. Even if you could have done it, you didn't. You hired someone else to think of it because it wasn't your expertise. Take the time to see what they are trying to show you before you dismiss it.

If you strongly believe though that your company's logo really demands an icon, here is some guidance that will help you immensely in your journey:

One of the most common problems that arises in icon development is the tendency to go overboard. Good icons are simple and easy to describe. Nike's icon is a "swoosh." One of our favorite icons was the Cingular "orange guy" (may he rest in peace). McDonald's has "golden arches."

But a lot of small business owners look at logos to be very literal and to contain a lot of information. When a client of ours in the mobile dog grooming business first came to us, his icon could only be described as "dog rolling in a soapy bathtub with wheels while washing his back." That's not an icon. It's a short story. When we re-concepted his logo, the icon we replaced it with was simply "wet pawprint" And it's a lot more iconic than the original could have ever been.

INSIDER'S TIP: Our rule of thumb is that if an icon can't be described in three words or less, it's too complicated. After all, if Ralph Lauren's icon was "well-dressed man on a horse wearing a striped shirt and sportcoat and hitting a ball with a polo mallet as he gallops through the field" instead of just "man on horse," how many people would want to wear that shirt?

The color(s) of success

What color is right for your business? You might hear your designer mention something about "color theory." It's the idea that certain colors have certain meanings. Green means "natural," blue means "relaxing," red means "danger," etc. But on the other hand, green is also a color associated with progress and technology, blue is strongly connected to health and healing and if red meant danger, Target might have thought differently about spending billions to brand with it.

So what do colors really say about your business? The real truth? Whatever you want them to. If someone tells you unequivocally that a certain color means a specific single thing, they're really saying that's what it means TO THEM. All our friends and colleagues know that Erik is a big fan of the color orange. We think it says smart, contemporary, and fresh. But some people feel differently about orange. Some people think it's retro, some people think it means safety. But what does it really mean? All these things and more — depending on the context.

How do you decide what colors work best in the context of your business? Here is our simple three-pronged strategy:

1. Whenever you're in doubt about any aspect of your brand, take off your "entrepreneur" hat and try to put yourself in your customer's shoes. It's extremely helpful to close your eyes and try to put together a mental image of a typical customer. Male or female? About how old? How much money do they make? What kind of car do they drive? How do they dress? Where do they shop? All those important things we talked about in the branding chapter.

Once you have a good mental picture, think about the color schemes that would connect with that person. Not getting anything? Think back to their clothes and their car. If you can see your customer wearing or driving a particular color, it's probably a good candidate. Is your customer a male executive that dresses mostly in gray business suits and drives a black or silver sedan? That wouldn't make for interesting design. In that case, look at his tie. Don't forget: even if your company sells business to business, BUSINESSES don't sign contracts. People do. At the end of the day, your audience is always people — no matter what you're selling.

2. Think about your product or service. Is there any range of colors that you should explore or eliminate strictly based on what you offer? For example, if you sell something that's organic or natural, it makes a lot of sense to look at colors commonly found in nature. If you sell a product or service that has to do with cleaning, you may want to stay away from colors that are dull or dark.

3. Only choose colors that you are comfortable with and don't let a designer push you around. They work for you and not vice versa. Respect them for showing you something gutsy or unconventional and for being passionate enough about their work to make a good case for it. But when it's all said and done, they need to listen to you if you're not comfortable with what you're seeing. You're the one that needs live with it, you're the one that needs to stand in front of the customer and present it. If you don't like it and can't feel passionate about it, you're doomed to changing it in the near future. Guaranteed.

And one last thing. If your business is personal to you, there is nothing wrong with choosing colors that have personal meaning. Unless they conflict directly with the nature of your audience or service, they will represent you well. You should always put pieces of yourself in your business wherever it makes sense. A color palette you love is just another one of those little things that can make you feel extra good about running your business — and anything that boosts your daily morale or gives you an extra shot of confidence when you're in front of a client will only contribute to your success.

INSIDER'S TIP: If color is something that you're very particular about, ask your design folks to show you the early concepts in black and white. That way you can judge the merit of the designs without having your opinions colored by the colors. As a side note, ANY logo you choose for your business should be able to work in black and white. If it doesn't look good in black and white, it's probably too complicated.

Rebranding: start from scratch or just refresh?

Kraft Foods unveiled a new logo recently only to have it panned harshly by snooty design types like us. Oh, and don't shed nostalgic tears for the old Kraft logo, this design change applies only at the corporate level. You won't be buying mac and cheese stamped with their new cluttered nonsense anytime soon. But before we judge too harshly, let's hear what Kraft CMO Mary Beth West had to say about the change (source, BrandWeek):

"In some ways, this really is all about Kraft Foods. It's about our next step in the evolution of getting ourselves to top-tier performance. Going forward, it defines, unifies, and simplifies our employees and gets everyone thinking about one common purpose."

Okay, so the new logo is going to make employees work harder and will unify them more than a decades-old American icon, known and loved by millions. Huh?

The point is that this is a crossroads that every mature company will one day come to: "We need to update our look before it gets completely dated. Do we wipe the slate clean and start from scratch or do we build on the equities we already have?"

Here's our answer: if the name, philosophy, products/services or values of a company change substantially then, yes — why not start from scratch? In any of these cases, you have little to gain by leveraging people's attachments to your old ideas. But otherwise, we usually prefer to refresh a look wherever possible and retain some of those "little details" that your customers recognize. You can refresh your image in the marketplace while preserving — and paying homage to — your heritage.

In contrast to the Kraft example, we were very pleasantly surprised when Toys R Us refreshed their look in 2007.

They did a great job, mostly because of the things they DIDN'T do:

- They didn't change their colors; the green and blue may have both gone a shade or two lighter, but no one except us strange design-folk would ever really notice that.

- They didn't change the shapes of their letters. The backwards "R" now has a star in the middle, but otherwise the letters seem exactly the same as they were 30 years ago.

- They didn't change the orientation of the logo or introduce a new icon or element.

All they did was make a few 2007 tweaks to an identity that has barely changed in decades. After all, when something has been around as long as Toys R Us, it's only natural that certain things start looking dated after a period of time. So every now and then, they "freshen" it up. Add a star, get rid of the star, adjust a color or two, get rid of those multi-colored facades and brown roofs that we remember from the '80s.

This strategy isn't unique to Toys R Us though. Remember how Delta changed their logo recently to the simplified red version? Remember how Apple took the rainbow stripes out of their famous icon late in the '90s? Look at the sleek new version of Intel's logo that is strikingly similar to the old one. Look around and you'll notice subtle but important changes in most of the brands you buy at the mall or use in your home.

So what can we learn from Toys R Us and other brands that have stood the test of time? That when our businesses start looking a little dated, we don't need to just sit back and live with it. And we don't necessarily need to wipe the slate clean and build something from scratch. That's a scary proposition for any business, especially a small business.

But it's a very low-risk proposition for you as a business-owner to take your logo to a good design firm and say, "I like my logo. It's represented my business well for 10 years and my customers know it. Can you show me some ideas on how I can contemporize it a little?" It shouldn't be an expensive project (no need to spend more than $700-900) and at the very least you're guaranteed to get a fresh perspective.

So for just a few hundred dollars every five years or so, your small business brand can evolve over time just like Toys R Us. Then your business will always look contemporary, dynamic, and relevant — never old or dated. It's a cheap and effective trick taken straight out of the big-business playbook.

So in looking back at Kraft Foods, they probably didn't need such a major change, especially if it's for the reasons West outlined in BrandWeek. We don't see any real redeeming qualities from a design perspective and have to imagine that the employees Kraft was trying to unite under this flag were scratching their heads as much the rest of us.

In fact, consider this: a lot of the negative response stemmed from the fear that the cluttered, garbled new logo was going to end up on the American cheese package, usurping a familiar icon. That feeling of loss must have been even worse at the corporate level being that not only do those employees know and use the products, but they actually help make, sell, and distribute them. If Kraft really felt it was time to update their corporate image we believe they would have been better served by staying closer to their original design.

How do I get good feedback on my new logo concept?

So it's the big day. You've been working with a design firm and you've just gotten your first logo concepts. Now what?

Many people's first impulse is to share, share, share. But it's not the best idea, especially when you're just looking at first concepts. Usually a designer will give you several ideas — probably three to five of them. The first thing you need to do is eliminate the concepts that you are completely uninterested in. Hopefully this narrows you to no more than 2 concepts.

Then, if you MUST share, choose one or two trusted advisers or colleagues. But make sure that they know your business almost as well as you do and that they understand what your design objectives are. Never show people graphic design "cold." You're likely to get the harshest and least constructive criticism in that scenario and it will confuse and frustrate you and may ultimately impact the design in a negative way.

The best time to show a design concept is when it's almost done and you just want some validation to seal the deal. But there are good ways and bad ways to do this. Don't present it and ask an open-ended question like "What do you think?"

Remember that most people aren't used to reviewing graphic design concepts and may not know how to best support you. And it goes without saying that when someone invites you to dole out criticism, a little switch goes off in your brain. We are inexplicably compelled to find something wrong with whatever it is that we're looking at and if we don't say something critical we're just not doing our jobs.

You'll hear everything from "it looks like a fish," to "I just don't like the color blue," to "We should add another big icon at the front and make everything bigger." If your concept is clean and modern, someone will tell you it looks retro. If you've done something traditional, someone will tell you it looks too contemporary. This feedback will get you nowhere.

So, when you do share, don't present open-ended invitation for critique. Say something like, "We've been working on a new logo and we think we're going to go with this one," or "Hey, look at our new logo." If people think the decision is already made, it takes the pressure off them to say something harsh. They're much more likely to tell you what they really think and you're actually likely to get compliments! And if someone really and truly doesn't like your logo design, they'll still tell you and probably give you a more valuable critique of why then they would have with an open-ended question.

Other tips:

- Don't show your whole office looking for comments, you'll get way too much feedback for any of it to be potentially valuable.

- Try to show only one person at a time. If you get a group together, you'll start to get a "leader and follower" group dynamic where one or two people give opinions and everyone else just nods their heads.

- Friends and family will almost always hate your design ideas and will be the most critical. We don't know why, but it's true. Be suspicious if they actually like what you're showing them. But if they rip you to shreds, run with the design — it's gold.

- You're the boss and don't forget it. It's YOUR company and YOUR vision. So don't ever let other people derail your ideas if you believe in them.

And one last tip. "I don't like it" is not good criticism. It doesn't help you and it doesn't help your designer. So if all someone can muster is "I don't like it" without a good reason or rationale, throw that comment out immediately and focus more on the feedback that has some real content.

Battle royale: the in-house design team vs. the hired help

Depending on what line of work you are in, your business may employ one or more full-time graphic designers. If so, you may have some special challenges to contend with ESPECIALLY if you hire an outside firm to spearhead the project.

During Erik's tenure as a corporate marketing manager, he was put in charge of an incredible project: the company was going to completely rebuild the look and feel of their flagship brand from the ground up and Erik would be in the driver's seat. This is the kind of project that marketing dorks like us drool over. But it was hard work. Turning words and ideas into something tangible always is.

Erik's team decided early on — based on a number of factors — that they would hire an outside agency to help with the design. The in-house design team was talented, but since they already had full-time roles, this project would be a secondary priority. And although the company had a lot of creative people, no one had much experience doing this kind of highly conceptual work.

As the project moved forward, Erik and his group would consult upper management and the in-house design folks every once in a while to share their progress and get their impressions. The work was good: Erik was happy and his executive team was happy. But the in-house designers just wouldn't warm up to what Erik's group was doing.

They were overly critical and sometimes they were even mean. Some of the in-house designers even took matters into their own hands, pulling executive and C-level employees into impromptu meetings in break rooms and offices where they would deconstruct the work Erik and his group had done, element by element, explaining all the reasons that it would fail and why the project should be scrapped immediately before it was too late.

Even though this is Erik's story, it probably sounds very familiar to many managers and business owners. This happens all the time when companies with in-house designers take their creative projects outside. "But it's just a business decision," most managers will say, "It's nothing against our design department."

That's probably true, but your design team probably doesn't

see it that way. We've worked with many designers and we know how they think. Creative people can be very sensitive when it comes to their work and tend to take things personally. In this type of situation, your designers may feel a little betrayed, they might feel passed over, or that you've lost your faith in them. A part of them will probably also feel that no matter what this other design group brings to the table, they could have done better. And so your in-house people can become predisposed — sometimes consciously but often subconsciously — to dislike the outside design group and their work.

This tension puts the people in charge of the project in an awkward situation. You want to keep your in-house team involved. You may need their buy-in and you probably want their advice throughout the process. But keeping them involved may derail your entire project. So how do you proceed?

We'd advise making your in-house designer part of the project team — don't let them be a spectator on the sidelines, waiting for their opportunity to make comments. Get them involved at the outset and put them in a position to speak directly to the outside firm in an advisory role. For example, have your designer speak to the outside firm about your web platform, your print production standards, the history of related projects, etc.

The more your in-house designers work with the outside designers, the more they'll feel like they're influencing the process and the more they may actually get to like the "outsiders." If they like the outside designers, they'll probably also respect them and may even learn from them. They'll feel like members of the team and will be more likely to give constructive feedback when it's time to review. It's also a benefit to the outside design team, who often comes into a project with little or no helpful history or context for a project. The internal designer can be a great resource for them and give them a unique perspective.

The only caution we would give is to make sure that your internal designer understands that creative control of the project lies with you. If they have any creative input they should come to you and let you filter that information for the outside designers. There's nothing more confusing for outside designers than getting conflicting creative direction from several parties at once.

As for the battle between marketing and the in-house design team from Erik's story, his team stuck to their guns and went with the design they wanted. The deciding vote ended up coming from the company's retail buyers who were given "sneak previews" at sales calls. The buyers loved the new design and company management went with it despite some of the internal protests. Erik was happy to have won his battle, but it's never good when a company spends several months fighting with itself. When the project was done, everyone had to work together again which wasn't easy at first.

It was shortsighted to try to make all of the decisions and expect the internal design group to get on board without a lot of involvement at the outset. At the same time, Erik's team was right not to cave when the objections started flying. They had done the work and knew it was right. And in a battle between a business team and a design team, the business team needs to win every time. It's a hard thing to say being someone with a design background but it's true. No designer — inside or outside — should be allowed to take the reigns of your business strategies away from you. No matter what happens during a creative project, make sure that you stay in control from start to finish.

Everything you ever wanted to know about designing a winning business card

Once you have a terrific logo, there's no better place to debut it than on a fantastic business card.

The first thing that everyone should know about business cards is that they are important. Very important. Oftentimes it's the first piece of printed marketing collateral we give out and it's also the piece likely to stay with the recipient longer than any other material you ever produce. The business card someone gives you today could end up in your rolodex, business card binder or file for years.

Postcards and brochures don't last that long, in fact we're lucky if they don't end up going straight into the trash.

A distinctive business card, one that reflects thought and effort, shows that you care about how your customers perceive you — that you want their respect and that you want to impress them. Cheap business cards don't impress anyone.

Do you have cheap business cards? You do if you answer "yes" to any of the questions below:

- Is your card printed on flimsy paper that can be easily folded, creased, or torn?

- Did you neglect to put a logo on your business card?

- Does your card have raised, gunky, rubbery lettering?

- Was your card designed using an online template wizard of some sort?

- Have you ever met someone at a networking function whose cards were almost indistinguishable from yours?

The classic rebuttal to the argument for distinctive business cards goes something like this: "But I want to get noticed for the quality of my work NOT because I have a fancy business card."

Consider this: Let's say you were a CPA. Your target audience — business owners and entrepreneurs — know LOTS of CPAs.

So let's say that we were in the market to hire a CPA (and this is purely hypothetical in the event our actual CPA is reading this). The first thing we would do is go back into our files and pull out the cards for all the CPAs we know. We're not saying that we evaluate people strictly on the quality of their business card. Obviously that isn't the case. But a business card does reflect the quality of the business and how much they care about what other people think of them. It will always play a role in a decision-making process whether consciously or subconsciously.

The same principal would apply if someone asked us to refer them to a good CPA. If we're going to hand out someone's card on their behalf, we're going to choose one that reflects our own standards. If your card doesn't look professional, what does that say about us when we give it to someone else?

So step one in having a great business card is to decide that it's important to you and that it will make a difference in your business. The next step is to partner with a designer or design firm. Be sure to request that at least one of your designs be a little "wild." Let the designer get creative. It's always easier to start with something wild and reel it in a little than it is to start with something conservative and then try to push the limits.

Unless you are a chronic business card note-taker, there is no reason NOT to go with a two-sided card. It's only a small investment in design and printing to do the second side and it makes a tiny piece of paper (just 2_ x 3.5_) twice as big. There is also no reason NOT to print your card in color.

The front of the card is for information. Keep it clean, simple, easy to read and — if your audience is corporate — easy to scan. Many of us who have tried usually learn the hard way that most business card scanners don't like white type on dark backgrounds. If you want to be scanner-friendly, go with a dark color on a light background. You don't have to do black type on a white card if you don't want to, but make sure you've got a lot of contrast.

The back of the card is for "wow." Add your marketing message, add some great imagery, or maybe just call attention to your URL if your web site is important to you.

Here are some business card "dont's":

- Don't overcrowd your card with information. No one wants to be overwhelmed with text or have to read 6 point type.

- If you have to put your picture on your card, try to do something creative or artistic with it. If you're in real estate or insurance or another industry where it's common to have your photo on your business card, imagine how much more your card would stand out from the crowd if it had a creative element to it and didn't just look like a drivers' license.

- Don't go for "gimmicky" cards. Rounded corners are okay, but squares, circles and odd sizes present problems for people that store cards in a business card portfolio or folder. It makes a GREAT presentation when you hand it to someone, but they are hard to keep. We got a business card from a design firm once that was a perfect square. It was cool and innovative, but got folded and mangled in our book. Now it looks like trash.

- Don't do anything you're uncomfortable with. You need a card that you'd be proud to hand out to anyone you meet. Yes, a business card is only seven square inches of paper, but they are likely the most important seven square inches in your entire marketing toolkit.

INSIDER'S TIP: In today's newfangledy world of digital printers, online printers, and bulk printers, you can get a thousand full-color, 2-sided business cards for less than $100. Sometimes considerably less than $100, depending on your source.

So why is this important? It creates a potentially valuable opportunity to make an additional impact at a low cost.

Many small business owners deal with several types of customers. Professional photographers, for example, often have both commercial and residential clients. And even within the residential segment, they may serve needs as varied as wedding photography, family portraits, and baby photography. You only have limited space on the back of the card to showcase examples of your work (2 - 3 shots maximum). And there's nothing worse than meeting a potential client and starting the discussion by explaining or apologizing for your business card because it doesn't look like you'd be a good choice for their project. So what do you do?

Easy. Get several different versions of your card. One card for commercial work — because commercial clients don't need to see any of your residential work, one card for weddings — because brides know there won't be a reshoot and want someone experienced — and one card for family portraits.

The same concept works for anyone that sells to several different kinds of customers and helps you get the reaction you want every time without alienating anyone. And at a networking event where you might meet lots of different people grab some of each card, shuffle the deck and hand them all out. It will be a testament to your versatility and make the experience of meeting you more memorable.

Designing your brochures + collateral

The first and best advice that we can offer about collateral design is to employ restraint. A lot of restraint.

When faced with a brochure or sales slick design project, a lot of business owners start to get nervous. We're paying a lot of money to design and print these things, so they have to be perfect. Understood. Loud. And clear. But when the business owner thinks about "perfect," a lot of us will stop seeing what's on the page and start focusing on what's NOT on the page. We didn't list all the features, should we talk about upgrades and our platinum package? Should we add information about our special promotion? How about all the in-use photos?

Yes, it's difficult, but if you're going to have a great looking brochure you have to learn to let these things go. But here's the good news, there actually is a marketing tool that you have at your disposal that has a virtually unlimited amount of space inside and that will allow you to list every little detail about your product, where you can have an entire photo gallery dedicated to every in-use shot you've ever done if you like. It's your website.

This is the 21st century now and the expectation that someone is going to make a purchase decision via brochure should be considerably reduced. The majority of your energy needs to be on your website — because anyone seriously considering doing business with you will end up there anyway and the role of your print materials should not be to make a sale, but to give your audience just enough information that they will want to go to the website to get the rest of the story.

Keep your print materials clean, simple, and beautiful. Don't get too wordy and don't get into any specifics that aren't absolutely necessary. The more in-depth you go, the faster your brochure is likely to become outdated and the more that will ultimately end up in the recycling bin.

Here are some basic guidelines for smart small business collateral in the digital age:

- Don't do anything too complex from a size/shape perspective. This kind of custom printing work can be expensive and you need to think with your wallet a little. You may spend five to ten times as much money to print a round or irregularly shaped brochure as it will cost to print just about any rectangular/square size with hard corners.

- Don't print a high quantity, only print what you need. It's more cost effective and better for the environment. If you need less than 1000 copies of something, look for a digital printer in your area — they specialize in small quantities.

- Avoid printing multiple page brochures whenever possible. With every page, you increase your risk exponentially that some piece of information will become dated, thereby ruining the entire book. If you can, print your collateral as a series of one page sales slicks. That way, if one sheet becomes dated, you only need to replace one sheet and not everything. Then print a simple generic pocket folder with your company logo on it and give the folder with whatever necessary sell sheets and materials to your client. If you do them right, you'll be able to use the folders for a couple of years.

- Note that this presentation model also gives you the ability to customize your collateral packet for each client, only showing them what they want or need to see. You can also include press releases, personal letters, and other relevant material in the folder; you'll find that little extra effort will be appreciated by your clients and prospects.

- Don't make your collateral too wordy. Most people don't want to read an essay about the product that someone just came to their office to pitch. Keep everything as simple and high-level as possible.

INSIDER'S TIP: Please, PLEASE don't print a trifold brochure. We all know why you like them — they are convenient to carry in a jacket pocket, they fit nicely into a counter stand for retail or a reception desk, they fit nicely into a regular letter-sized envelope for mailing and wow — it's only one piece of paper!

But here's the problem: a trifold brochure is actually a six-page brochure printed on one piece of paper. That means that we're trying to cram three times as much information as there should be on each side.

They aren't easy to design and they are even more difficult for our audience to read and actually follow.

If you want all the pluses of a trifold brochure without any of the problems, we usually advise just doing an 8.5" x 3.5" postcard. You won't have the real estate to overload your audience, they can be printed more cheaply than trifolds, and still fit in your jacket pocket, in the brochure stand and the letter-sized envelope. Remember, we only have to provide JUST enough information to get someone to the website. That's all.

How do you hire the right design firm?

As we have discussed here at length, the quality of your marketing materials is essential. When you meet with a potential client, these are the items that they are going to use to judge your quality as a vendor. Poorly made business cards or a template website will not get the right message across and will not impress anyone. Unless you have a background in graphic design and marketing communications, do NOT try to put these materials together yourself with DIY tools. Similarly, don't try teaching yourself Adobe Illustrator, Photoshop, or Dreamweaver, and don't hire a cousin/ neighbor's kid/college student, etc. to work on your critical marketing materials.

Hire a reputable firm to work on your core materials and be sure that you look hard for the right fit. That can be easier said than done though, so here are some tips to help you find the right design partner:

Do your homework before you engage or even interview. A good design firm will ask you about what makes your brand "tick"" beneath the surface. Prepare notes about your brand and a positioning statement or mission statement. Provide your tagline. Write down as many details as possible about what you're looking to achieve visually. Do you think your brand demands a more contemporary or traditional style? Is it important to you to have a logo with a distinctive icon in it? Are there other logos or websites out there that inspire you? Who are your competitors? Good design rarely happens in a vacuum and preparing for the design process is key. A lot of experienced marketers will tell you that this preparation has a much greater impact on your success in a design project than your choice of a design firm.

If you don't have the time to flesh this out before meeting with a design firm, look for a firm that offers branding expertise as well as design. You could also look for an independent consultant but be prepared to pay for some of their time. A "free consultation" or "free assessment" will not get your project the attention it needs.

Budget is important. Obviously, as a small business owner, you are going to be sensitive to monetary concerns.

Don't go with anyone that promises you the best price or a significant discount. You will get what you pay for. A better policy is to go with a firm that will guarantee a maximum budget, provided of course that the scope of work does not increase. Without some sort of guarantee in this regard, be prepared to spend about 30% more than what you were quoted. Not that design firms always overcharge, but additional revisions, meetings, etc. can add up quickly. It's also helpful to go into the process with at least a vague idea of what you're willing to spend.

Make sure you can work together. Discuss the process and design methodology ahead of time and make sure that the workflow of the project is compatible with your schedule. For example, most small business owners have trouble scheduling regular meetings during the business day and don't like taking business hours away from customers. If that's the case, look for a firm that has an established online workflow where projects and approvals can be managed largely over the web. If a project becomes a pain to manage from your perspective, it's likely to get off track quickly.

Check their work. When evaluating a portfolio, look for diversity in clients and in visual styles. Don't saddle yourself with a "one-trick pony." If all the work in their portfolio looks similar or all uses a common visual style, it's a fair bet that the work they do for you will come out like everything else in their portfolio. Some firms have a lot of range though, so hold out for a firm that can adapt their style to your vision.

Generalist or specialist? It's usually best to stay away from industry "specialists." When a company makes it's entire living serving a single industry or vertical, that's often a red flag for small business owners. If a firm claims to know everything about marketing for CPA firms or restaurants, it usually means they have a premade formula they are likely to stick to regardless of the specific needs of your business. It also means that as soon as they get done working with you, they'll usually sell the same service to one of your competitors. Differentiation in a marketplace comes from having a fresh perspective, not the same ideas and the same advisors and designers as your competition.

Remember that a relationship with a design or marketing firm is a partnership. They will NEVER know as much about your business as you do. Likewise, most small business owners lack the experience and/or objectivity to effectively direct high-level marketing/branding/design initiatives. Find common ground between your experiences and things should go very well.

CONTROVERSIAL TOPICS:
Discount design and crowdsourcing

Everyone wants to save a little money here and there, no question about it. But is design the right place to do it? In recent years we've seen the emergence of two controversial trends in commercial design: discounters and crowdsourcing.

Discount Design

"Discounters" exist primarily online, offering clients the opportunity to purchase logos and other design services for outrageously low fees, prices that no reputable/competent designer or firm could possibly compete with and stay in business. A companion to the discount sites are the "freelance auction" sites like Guru.com where clients post RFPs and designers bid for the work (with the job presumably being awarded to the lowest bidder).

Designers everywhere are outraged by the idea that purchase decisions on design are being made primarily on the basis of price. The low-price leaders get the business and the true artists feel that they are being slowly crowded out of their own business by anonymous, less-experienced designers who are happily working for cheap. The established graphic designers and design houses are afraid that over time, this "price first" sensibility is going to destroy their livelihood.

We tend to disagree on this point. There will always be a need for a wide variety of price ranges in graphic design, just like Target needs a wide variety of price points in the coffee maker aisle. Some customers will want bargain basement, but some customers are looking for a premium experience. The difference between coffee makers and graphic design is that people have always known how to get a cheap coffee maker. And the manufacturers of high-end, fancy coffee makers always knew that there were other companies out there making cheap coffee makers that weren't as nice, weren't as durable, and weren't as feature-rich.

Until a few years ago when sites like ebay and Priceline set the stage for other flavors of "bid what you'll pay" or "name your own price" online communities, most design firms didn't even understand how large a marketplace there was for low-cost design. A lot of people are still stunned by the fact that someone will go to a website and hire a stranger to design their logo for $75. Or even worse, design their OWN logo with an online wizard for $50. But the truth is, these people were ALWAYS out there. There has always been a very receptive market for discount graphic design and there has always been a group of providers that were willing to give it to them. The only difference between then and now is that a fast-maturing and increasingly visible online marketplace is calling attention to a segment of the industry that was always marginalized and ignored by the establishment.

Here's our feeling: people with disposable income who truly appreciate the experience of driving will buy a Mercedes or a Porsche. People who just want to get from point A to point B on a tight budget will buy a Hyundai or a Chevy. And there are plenty of Toyotas, Volkswagens, and Acuras in between. Likewise, companies with big budgets that like the experience of working with big agencies will go that route, companies who don't see the value of graphic design but need something to put on their business card will look for a bargain. Have a small-to-mid range budget but big aspirations? That company will probably go with an established small design firm.

We really don't see customers moving en masse to the cheapest solution they can find. In fact, in our experience, it's more of a rebound effect where customers try a discount design firm or cheap freelancer and don't get what they were looking for. Then they bounce back up to a firm like ours. Sometimes you need to be disappointed in something cheap in order to appreciate the value of quality.

So does discount design hurt the industry? In our opinion, only if the good designers out there let discounters get the better of them. Our business is changing and more designers need to embrace that as a challenge to break conventions that have been in place for decades. We're just experiencing now what many industries have already seen as online shopping has evolved from a novelty to a way of life. Businesses that try to buck that trend don't usually fare well and the same goes here.

But is discount design good for the client? No, not from what we've seen. If you truly don't have more than $100 to spend on a logo, we'd much rather see you go to a discounter than start up Microsoft PowerPoint and try to take matters into your own hands. But that situation notwithstanding, there's no good reason to use a discounter. All you are likely to get is a shotgun approach to your design without any real strategy behind it. There are differing opinions on this matter, but we can only speak from our experience and can say very honestly that our firm has made a lot of money over the years from clients asking us to replace the sloppy work that they had done on the cheap.

Crowdsourcing

Crowdsourcing is a phenomenon that has become increasingly common in a wide variety of industries now that online collaboration is so easy. Essentially the principle behind crowdsourcing is that a company will post the details of a design project on a facilitating website, outline what they are looking for, and what they are willing to pay. Designers then post their design concepts to the site. The client may request revisions on design concepts, and if they are satisfied, they select one.

Sounds pretty straight forward, right? Sure, but here's the twist and why the design community is so up in arms about this: Only the "winning" designer makes any money at all. When designers submit work to a crowdsourced design site, they should not have ANY expectation of earning money for their work. In the industry, we call this "spec" (or speculation) work and there is an unofficial — though widely accepted — belief that freelance designers shouldn't be doing spec work and that, as professionals, they should be paid fairly for their efforts.

We recently had an experience with a client who had just crowdsourced their new logo. They opened the project on a website along with a description of what they were looking for and the promise of a few hundred dollars to be awarded to the guy or gal who contributed the winning logo. They received more than 40 submissions in a matter of days from about 20 different designers.

Before we go on however, Erik would like to freely disclaim that he used to run a corporate marketing communications department and, while serving there, did on occasion ask for sample designs prior to the start of any formal engagement with no expectation of payment. But he asked this only from agencies and only on large projects like major web design initiatives.

When a company does that kind of shopping, they are looking to develop a long-term relationship with a brand name agency that will ultimately be able to earn several hundred thousand to several million dollars or more in revenue over the life of their engagement with the client. Asking that the agency contribute a couple thousand dollars in man hours as an initial investment is both reasonable and justified.

This, however, is not what happens in a crowdsourced design project. 20-50 relatively anonymous freelance designers (identified only by their online handle) may submit in the hopes that they will earn a prize of a few hundred dollars and are then unlikely to hear from the client ever again. In our case, the client we mentioned earlier had already awarded us their web design project before they had even notified the winner of the logo project. And there is just something ethically wrong with asking a (virtual) room full of people to each perform a service that is worth several hundred dollars on the condition that only one of them will actually be paid for their efforts.

So here's our opinion on the virtues of crowdsourcing from a client's point of view: don't do it, it is NOT to your advantage. You are participating in an environment where designers have to "play the odds" to decide how hard they will work on a particular concept and a high value is placed from a designer's point of view on the quantity of submissions rather than their quality.

You are NOT getting an audience with someone who will take the time to learn your business before attempting to design for it, you are NOT paying for a designer's undivided attention and you are NOT engaging in a relationship with someone who cares about (or who stands to benefit from) the success of your business.

All you are getting is a shotgun blast of quick design work from designers who are throwing as much out as they can, trying to play the odds and make something stick. From your perspective as a client, you're just throwing the dice and hoping that something usable comes out of it. Unless you truly see design as a commodity and don't see any value in working with someone who will approach your project strategically, crowdsourcing just doesn't make a bit of sense from a business owner's point of view.

As for our client who crowdsourced their logo before they engaged with us on the web design, they got lucky. There was a single shining diamond among a batch of poorly-conceived work and their new logo is actually pretty nice. Out of curiosity though, we clicked on the profile of the person who created it and noticed that the concept for the winning design had been lifted from another design they had presented (and won) a couple of weeks earlier for a different client.

But that's probably just the nature of the game.

INSIDER'S TIP: The bottom line here is that you get what you pay for in design as with anything else. And especially when you factor in the cost of being dissatisfied, you realize that it doesn't cost anything extra to get good design from the start. And when we talk about the "cost of dissatisfaction," we're not just referring to money. Consider also how much longer it will take you to get that design you want if you have to redo it three times and the hours that you will spend personally trying to manage the process. Consider also the embarrassment of either having to go to market with a look you are not proud of or having to delay a launch because you are simply not ready.

Give your work to someone you can actually develop a relationship with, someone who stands to benefit from your success. Discounters and crowdsourcing can't offer that. And while we don't believe that crowdsourcing is unethical, it is a gray area and it's something that as business owners we would probably stay away from. When you crowdsource, your project is public and you may not want to involve your company in the controversy and risk alienating your firm from the local design base.

Chapter three

Small business marketing planning that works

In this chapter, we're going to help you attack your marketing plan with a logical, organized approach that is designed to produce results at every stage. Over time, this process will help you maintain an effective, integrated marketing strategy that actually works.

As you will see, our framework organizes the marketing approach into six layers, all of which serve a different purpose in your overall strategy. We recommend implementing them in the order that we have given them — not necessarily because one thing should always come before the other — but because we acknowledge that most small business owners don't have the time, human resources, or budget to implement a big plan in a short period of time.

Our framework also helps you prioritize your marketing initiatives in a logical fashion. This allows for pieces to build on one another rather than trying to create several initiatives all in isolation. Prioritization is absolutely crucial to small business marketing success. Most entrepreneurs have no shortage of good ideas; we get them all day long and sometimes in our sleep — we are also constantly deluged by friends, family, and colleagues who are always offering input and "surefire" paths to success. If you were to list out all these ideas and opportunities you'll quickly find yourself overwhelmed. Knowing when to "say when" to the constant influx of ideas and stay focused on a plan is critical — and hopefully this chapter will help you make those decisions.

The small business marketing problem

No one teaches small business owners how to build an effective marketing plan and unfortunately, only a gifted few are actually born with a seemingly innate gift for marketing greatness. Consider Steve Jobs and Richard Branson, for example.

Those of us that attended business school or were part of an MBA program will likely remember our marketing communications classes as highly theoretical and centered around successful strategies used by big businesses. Many of the highly regarded books out there have the same fundamental problem: techniques and strategies built around big budgets and a reliance on mass media advertising.

Erik had a marketing professor in his MBA program who said, "The more you advertise, the more you will sell."

That may be true in the world of mass-retailer consumer goods — where you can afford to spend millions to infiltrate people's minds with ubiquitous advertising— but it isn't true for the small business owner where budgets are low and opportunity costs are sky high.

One of the first lessons you'll learn in any fundamental marketing communications book or class is that marketing is a science of Reach times Frequency. Or, "How many people are seeing my ad and how many times are they seeing it?" What isn't intuitive about the Reach x Frequency formula however, is that Frequency is the more important variable of the two. I will sell more of my product if I reach 20 people 10 times each than if I were to reach 200 people only once.

That is why advertising doesn't work for the majority of small businesses out there. Because entrepreneurs usually don't have the budget to reach their targets enough times and in enough different media to make it meaningful — to get inside people's minds. The other thing that small businesses don't realize about mass media advertising is that it's terribly wasteful. Big businesses can afford this waste, but small businesses cannot. For example, in your local community magazine, your ad can probably be seen by 10,000 - 20,000 people every week. But how many of those 20,000 are really ideal customers for you? It likely isn't 20,000. And, taken on its own, independent of a bigger strategy, most small business owners can count the number of times that local print advertising made their phone ring on one hand.

What most of the ad reps don't tell you is that the beauty of advertising isn't in influencing sales directly — it's in the visibility it gives you in the community. This ultimately leads to credibility, which ultimately leads to sales. It isn't a direct cause and effect relationship. As most of us will recognize from our own experiences in shopping nowadays, our culture has moved from "yellow pages" types of purchases where we learn about a service provider and then promptly call and hire them. We now solicit referrals from friends, family, and colleagues; socialize our purchase decisions on Facebook and Twitter; and use vendors' websites to validate our decisions. Simply knowing a service provider exists is no longer enough to substantially effect a purchase decision.

So when the ad rep tells you that advertising is going to get you sales, they aren't exactly lying... they're just exaggerating. At the end of the day, you're not buying a sales pipeline when you advertise in your local newspaper or magazine — you're buying visibility.

Steve Tingris, CEO and founder of Enthusem.com, a web startup with a new angle on direct mail says, "In the days of what I call 'funnel marketing' you would put out 100 messages to get 10 or 20 people to respond. I think those days are coming to an end though because now individuals are getting so many marketing messages that the ratios aren't holding. Imagine turning the funnel upside-down. Rather than mailing to a lot of people to get one response, we've seen success where business owners target just a few really perfect prospects for great success."

Marketing a small business just isn't as simple as writing a check for advertising. It takes ingenuity, determination, and elbow grease.

We don't want to suggest that spending on advertising is always a mistake — it depends on how you're using it and the difference you believe it will make for your business. But the "myth" of advertising is a problem for entrepreneurs and creates false expectations for business owners who don't know where to start with their marketing planning.

INSIDER'S TIP: Talk to a group of successful small business owners and ask them where they get the majority of their business. At least eight out of the ten will tell you that the secret to their success isn't the Internet, direct mail, or the local newspaper. It's referrals and gateopeners, those connections who may never become a client, but who have the ability to refer you to many qualified prospects.

It's not sexy and it sure as heck isn't the "get rich quick scheme" that a lot of advertising sales reps promise when they tell you to invest your entire budget in whatever they're selling.

There are no shortcuts in marketing, just as there are no shortcuts anywhere in your business. There is no magic silver bullet that you can invest in to suddenly make your phone ring off the hook with qualified prospective business.

What's the difference between marketing + advertising?

Earlier this year, Erik was speaking at an event and was asked what the difference between marketing and advertising was. It was a fantastic question — as many business owners use the two terms almost interchangeably — and a great way to dig into the topic of small business marketing.

First, let's address the terminology. If you ever have a question about what a marketing term means, make yourself look smart by visiting the extensive marketing dictionary available on the American Marketing Association's website.

Here is how the AMA defines marketing:

"Marketing is an organizational function and a set of processes for creating, communicating, and delivering value to customers and for managing customer relationships in ways that benefit the organization and its stakeholders."

This, by contrast, is the textbook definition of advertising:

"The placement of announcements and persuasive messages in time or space purchased in any of the mass media by business firms, nonprofit organizations, government agencies, and individuals who seek to inform and/or persuade members of a particular target market or audience about their products, services, organizations, or ideas."

So what does it mean? First off, marketing is BIGGER. It encompasses value and managing customer relationships in addition to advertising. Marketing is also strategic while advertising is tactical.

Most importantly though — especially from a small business perspective — is that advertising is PASSIVE. You put your message in front of as many eyeballs as you can afford and wait for the customer to make the next move. However, marketing is an ACTIVE process by which you determine how you are going to reach your customers, persuade them to purchase from you and, after the purchase, make them happy.

The passive, impersonal nature of advertising — along with the staggeringly poor ROI — usually makes it a poor investment for small business owners (unless it is meant as a brand awareness-builder to support an existing and ongoing campaign). However, ALL entrepreneurs need to build winning marketing strategies in order to compete effectively during tough economic times.

Focusing on value, message, experience, and brand are all great ideas that can positively influence your company's sales. And you didn't even need to advertise. Now we'll show you how.

The small business marketing model

This is the part that takes imagination. But hey, marketing requires a little creativity so bear with us on this, it'll be worth your while.

Imagine your business as a small planet floating in space. Your planet has an atmosphere and gravity. Your prospects float in the air above you and you make sales on the surface. The closer to The Surface your prospects come, the "warmer" they are, the easier it is to sell them and the higher your ROI on any marketing initiatives you use to close them. By contrast, the further away from The Surface someone is, the more expensive it is to market to them and the harder it is to close them. If you're going to pick fresh fruit, strawberries are easier to get to than apples and apples are a whole lot easier to get to than coconuts. Same idea here.

The warm referral sent by one of your current customers is very close to The Surface. With their friend's endorsement, they are already well on their way to doing business with you before they even contact you. The people reading your magazine ad or driving by your billboard, however, are strangers — it will take a lot of work to educate that person and make them a customer.

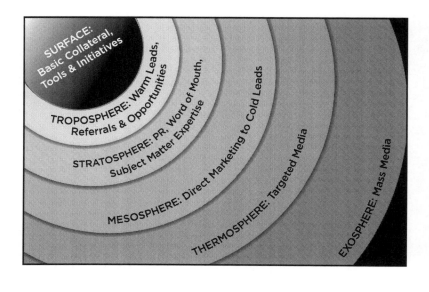

Our chart outlines how a small business marketing plan should be organized, with the marketing initiatives categorized within different layers, and ordered from left to right in terms of:

1. Where your marketing priorities should be and the order they should be rolled out

2. The relative cost to maintain them (though each layer has it's own startup costs in terms of time and money investment)

3. Your chances of making a sale as a direct result of your work

Each layer builds on the last, giving you the tools you need to be successful in the next. For example, there is little sense in doing any direct marketing if you don't have a mechanism in place for closing opportunities that are already warm.

A successful small business marketing strategy will begin with the fundamental tools — the ones on The Surface — and then build outward starting with the initiatives necessary to optimize and create the warm opportunities (and then close them) and ultimately finishing — if necessary or beneficial — with mass advertising.

The Surface

This is where the action happens. The Surface is where we connect our brand with our leads and opportunities. Of all the components of your marketing program, The Surface is arguably the most important because it's where you actually CLOSE business and supports everything else you do. The quality of your marketing program quickly becomes irrelevant if you don't have the right tools in place to win some of the opportunities that come through the door.

This layer is where you keep all your basic marketing tools and assets: your logo, your business cards, your company website, your PowerPoint presentation, your brochure, and other basic marketing collateral.

As we've already discussed at length in the design and web chapters, the quality of your marketing tools is pretty darn important. When you meet with a potential client, these materials will reflect on your quality as a vendor. Poorly made business cards or a template website will not get the right message across and will not impress anyone. Unless you have a background in graphic design and marketing communications, do NOT try to put these materials together yourself with DIY tools — they will never turn out as you hoped. Similarly, don't try teaching yourself Adobe Illustrator, Photoshop, and DreamWeaver and don't hire a cousin/neighbor's kid/college student, etc. to work on your critical marketing materials.

These elements are important to your business and —
unless you have the skill to do this job better than an outside
agency or professional — it is not a good use of your time
and it will take you several times longer to muddle through
than an experienced designer.

There are other key elements to The Surface beyond
the high-profile elements that need to be professionally
designed. They make a big difference though. These
elements include:

• **Email signatures:** What do they say? Is it just your
name, phone number, and web address (i.e., info that
most people you email already have) or are you using it to
add value like inviting your contacts to connect with you
on Twitter or LinkedIn — things they may not have done
or thought to do previously. If you are rolling out a new
product or service, why not add a bit of text or an image
nudging people to ask you about it the next time you talk.

• **Phone and voicemail greetings:** These bring the same
kinds of opportunities as email signatures but also offer
additional opportunities to do something fun and unexpected.
For example, if you call the Zero-G Creative office (888-538-
1466) and press just about any extension, you'll discover
that Erik — along with another tone-deaf vocalist from the
office — actually sing our own hold music. Fortunately,
we're a marketing agency and not a software consultancy
or a law firm. But as silly as it is, it is unexpected and a fun

conversation starter when one of us picks up the phone. No need to get locked in to "Hi, thanks for calling. I'm not in right now, but if you'll leave me a message along with your name and number I will get back to you just as soon as I can."

• **How callers are greeted by a "live" receptionist (or by whoever is answering the phone):** If you do have a live person answering your phone, that may very well be the first live interaction a potential lead has with your company. Treat it like the opportunity it is.

• **Proposal templates and written correspondence:** When you send a document to a client, how much of your brand comes across? How is it personalized for your audience? Is it straight facts or does it relate somehow to the overall experience you want to create for a client? Again, it goes without saying that taking this idea to its creative conclusion may not be appropriate in certain business environments, but bottom line there's almost always something you can improve here.

• **ANYTHING else that a customer or prospect may come into direct contact with in the bid or customer service process:** Did we miss anything? Just stay true to your branding objectives and take a good hard look at anything and everything that touches the client or leads directly and you will be fine.

The Surface is where you win business. Make sure you devote enough time and attention to building it well.

INSIDER'S TIP: Consider what you actually need in the way of marketing materials before you go too far down the road and create materials you don't need. Does anyone care if you leave them a big folder full of material or is your audience unlikely to be impressed by such an effort? Do you need a fancy proposal template or does it make more sense to submit estimates by email? Consider your audience and your goals carefully. Choosing the right materials to keep in your arsenal is as important as executing them well.

Troposphere: warm leads, referrals, + opportunities

These people are closest to The Surface and are — by the laws of gravity in our small business marketing model — the leads and prospects that are going to be the cheapest to sell to and the ones that you are most likely to close. Once you've got the right tools at The Surface, focus on building opportunities in this space before engaging in any other marketing initiatives.

Here are a few things to consider:

Your "Birth Announcement": The first thing we recommend when you're open for business is to let all of your friends, family, and business associates know that you've struck out on your own and tell them briefly about your business. One of our associates calls this a "Birth Announcement" which is an appropriate and memorable way to describe this.

Send out yours via email or by a note in the mail. It doesn't have to be long and it doesn't need fancy graphics. Make it part of your standard operating procedure to do this every time you announce a new product, service, or business extension. If you're going to build a strong referral base, family, friends, and past/present business partners are a fantastic place to start as they are the people who know you best and are most likely on day one to start sending you business. Keep them informed! Make this the start of a constantly-building email list that you follow up with an email or newsletter at least once a quarter.

Network, Network, Network: Networking is critical as it not only gives you the opportunity to make new connections on a personal one-on-one basis, but also helps you demonstrate that you are passionate and engaged in your business and active in the business community.

As with all things though, it is also important to be strategic about it. You will meet all types of people out there and a lot of people will be more than happy to take your business card and invite you to coffee. But don't expect to make customers out of all those people. Many will be "tire-kickers" who are not ready to make a purchase decision. Some will imply a greater interest in your service than they actually have in order to facilitate a private meeting where they can try to push their wares on you. Be selective about who you "do" coffee or lunch with. If you believe they may be a good lead for you, try to qualify them first. It is very easy to get bogged down in appointments. This is not a winning strategy.

The most efficient way to network is to actively search for gate openers and save your coffee and lunch appointments for them. "Gate openers" is a term that you'll commonly find in networking circles and it describes a person that is not likely to become your customer, but is in a position to refer a lot of business to you. For example, we are in the small business marketing and graphic design business. Good gate openers for us are business coaches and CPAs who serve the same types of clients that we do. Marketing consultants, PR people, and copywriters are also good gate openers as they often need help with their own accounts. If you're going to spend an hour with someone in a coffeehouse, it may as well be someone that can get you 10 clients as opposed to just one.

INSIDER'S TIP: Taryn Pisaneschi, an Atlanta-based networking expert, has a lot of terrific advice on successful networking habits:

"People forget to connect with each other. They go to events all the time, they hand out cards, and they forget to ask, 'Who are you? What are some of your favorite things? How did you get into this business?' It's one of the networking fundamentals that people forget about, which is give, give, give and THEN you will get," Taryn says.

"To ensure success when networking, set a goal. Think ahead of time about who you are looking to meet and aim to meet two to three quality people. Spend a couple of minutes with each person and when you follow up with them, reference your conversation, and try to be a resource. When people talk to you, they often share problems. It could be 'My business is hurting because of the economy,' it could be, 'I had a hard day at work,' it could be, 'I'm about to be let go.' If you listen for those pain words, you can become a resource. And when you help someone solve a problem, they are going to be more interested in what you have to say."

Sell to the People You Know: Another important — though often overlooked — part of a successful referral marketing program is continued marketing to existing customers. Email newsletters and periodic mailed note cards are great ways to facilitate this, providing two big benefits. The first is the opportunity to win incremental business from current and past customers. It is ALWAYS cheaper to sell to people you know than to people you don't.

The second benefit is the opportunity to solicit endorsements and referrals. Letters of recommendations and case studies are infinitely useful as marketing tools.

Your customer base is also a powerful source for referrals. You may consider putting an official referral program in place where you monetize referrals that become customers either in cash or gifts or in exchange for credits/discounts towards your product or service. Different people have different levels of comfort with paying for referrals so do whatever feels appropriate in this regard. Whether or not there's compensation or discounting involved, make sure that you tap this resource early and often.

Stratosphere: PR, word of mouth, + subject matter expertise

If you've become adept at converting warm leads into paying customers, you're likely to start thinking to yourself,

"This is fantastic! Now where can I get more?"

The reality is that there's only so far you can go with networking and referral programs alone. Although very profitable, networking is extremely time intensive and you'll find that there's a practical limit to the number of hours that you can commit to it on a weekly basis — especially once you factor in the time spent doing follow-ups, lunches, coffees, etc.

So how do you go about finding more people that are already interested in YOU before you even speak to them?

The answer is up in the Stratosphere and it involves increasing your exposure sphere of influence beyond networking alone and leveraging your company's news and expertise to build awareness and interest in your business without a large cash outlay. You are likely to notice that many of the initiatives and opportunities described here are either wholly online or in connection with the Internet. Why? Because being found or otherwise recommended online can be almost as good as a documented "official" referral. Prospects that find you via tools like these may not actually know you, but they will feel like they do.

Below are some components that you might consider when building a strategy:

Public Relations: There is a lot more to PR than what we'll go into here, but regular press releases are a great (and affordable) place to start in the absence of an active PR strategy if you're not ready to bring on a consultant or small agency on a monthly basis.

Have an exciting new customer, product, or service? Write a press release. Exhibiting or speaking at an event or trade show? Write a press release. Have tips or information that potential customers or other business owners might benefit from? Write a press release.

Developing a news stream is not difficult and can be invaluable for your business. Not sure how to get started? Just Google "How do I write a Press Release?" and you will get lots of good information.

Be sure to publish all your releases on your website and distribute on the web. There are paid services like PRWeb and PRNewswire that you can explore as well as a few free options. You may also want to invest some time in compiling the names of reporters and editors of local papers and sending to them as well. If you are a member of a local Chamber of Commerce, they may also be willing to publish your announcement in their newsletter or on their website.

If you have the means to work with a legitimate PR professional (not all of them are outrageously expensive) you will likely benefit a great deal. Anyone can write a press release, but the real value of working regularly with an outside PR person is in having an experienced pro actively pitching story ideas to the media and giving you another sounding board from a marketing perspective.

INSIDER'S TIP: If your idea of "PR" is writing a press release and distributing it on the wire, that's fine. Consider it a "stay in touch" strategy with the world and enjoy the Search Engine Optimization benefits associated with having additional information about your company on the web. But don't expect any reporters to call you out of the blue. While the new low-cost and free press release distribution tools has made the press release process faster and more cost-effective, it has also increased the number of press releases being distributed on a day-to-day basis, making it impossible for reporters to stay in touch. Simultaneously, economic woes and the maturation of the online news industry seem to have also dwindled the number of traditional reporters out there. If your goal is to actually be interviewed or featured in a major news outlet, get a PR person.

Blogging: Why not start a blog? It's fun, easy, and a great way to demonstrate your knowledge and experience. As an added bonus, search engines love blogs, so having one gives you additional opportunities online.

The biggest fear that most business owners have about starting a blog? Keeping up with it. People often have the misconception about blogging that they have to do it every day or several times a week. A few times a month is definitely sufficient though. And blog posts don't have to be long. A few informative sentences are usually sufficient. Most blog software will also allow you to load your posts before you publish them. We recommend that business owners spend a day every couple of months and write a LOT of posts so they can preload the system with a month to a quarter's worth of content all at once. Then just set calendar reminders for yourself to periodically publish them.

Be sure to also create a "blogroll" by linking to your favorite blogs and asking the owners of those blogs to link back to you. This will allow you meet other experts in your field and may (search experts we speak to are torn on this point) help generate better search engine rankings for your blog.

Not sure you can really get the hang of the blogging thing? A great way to practice is by leaving comments on other people's blogs. It's a small time investment and a pretty easy way to get used to writing conversationally about business topics.

Social Networking: There are many ways to flex your expertise online beyond blogging. Facebook, LinkedIn,

Twitter, and other networking sites are great places to connect with other business owners and potential prospects as well as to solicit endorsements from past customers and business partners.

LinkedIn and Twitter create especially interesting opportunities as you have the opportunity to ask your connections for introductions to gate openers and potential clients in their network.

Your profiles on social networking sites can also help you improve your search engine ranking. We won't give you too much detail here — there's a whole social media chapter later in the book for you to sink your teeth into.

Speaking Engagements: There are very few ways more powerful to demonstrate your knowledge and expertise than to give a live presentation. If you don't know where to look for these types of opportunities, try talking to business associates who are members of trade organizations, philanthropy groups, social clubs, or networking groups.

You might also consider talking to owners of businesses and venues that cater to your core audience. You could also ask them if they'd be willing to let you use their location for a talk. If they think their customers will benefit or if they think they can get a lot of people in the door, they may agree. Ask them to promote the event to their customers and you can promote it to your email list. Be sure to publish a press release and a notice on your website, too.

Here are some helpful tips for giving a good presentation:

- A lot of people are uncomfortable speaking for an audience. If this is you, it's natural to be nervous but don't let it get to you. Do everything you can to make yourself comfortable. Wear clothes that don't make you self-conscious and don't wear uncomfortable shoes — speak conversationally and engage the audience as you would during a one-on-one presentation. And most of all — *be yourself.*

- Serve food. Coffee and snacks are great and we've also seen some good presentations given over lunch. If your audience is hungry, they will have a hard time focusing.

- PREPARE. Don't come in cold without practicing. You need to know your material inside and out. If you're unprepared, people will see it.

- Bring visual aids. Projectors and PowerPoint presentations are great, but if that isn't your style, bring a whiteboard or an easel with a pad. Visual aids help the audience maintain their focus.

- If you do a PowerPoint, be sure that you resist the temptation to write an essay on each slide — people won't be able to read it all and if they try, it will divert their attention from what you are saying. *Use a lot of pictures and don't put more than 10 words on each slide.*

- Bring handouts. Nothing fancy and nothing too marketing-oriented but something that your audience can take home or to their office and refer to. Mention your website and other resource links relevant to your talk that may be available on your site. Also be sure to clip one of your business cards to every handout.

- Do NOT make a sales pitch. Make sure that the audience understands who you are, who you represent, and what your company does. But keep your actual presentation informative. If they feel like they are being sold, they will tune out. Instead, give them helpful information, and tell them things that they may not know. If you give a good talk and get your audience interested, you'll find that a lot of selling opportunities — and additional speaking opportunities — will be sure to follow.

- Be brief. Try to keep the whole presentation — including question and answer time — within about an hour.

One last idea on speaking. Set up a video camera at the venue if possible and record your presentation. You may be uncomfortable watching yourself, but you're sure to learn a thing or two about how you can improve. And while you're at it, post the video on your website, pull out the audio and podcast it or trim it down under 10 minutes and post it on YouTube. You've got great content, so make it as available as possible.

INSIDER'S TIP: Webinars are also a great way to present your content without having to get up in front of a room of people. However, you need to be careful in choosing a good online presentation platform. Make sure that you test your online presentation tool on several people (preferably as technically unsavvy as possible) to make sure that you don't spend the first 20 minutes of your presentation time trying to make sure everyone can see your intro slide. These kinds of setbacks can be VERY embarrassing to you and frustrating to attendees, which is not the kind of impression you will want to leave.

White Papers + eBooks: Yes, people do read these. White papers are a great way to demonstrate your familiarity with a topic and your ability to solve particular types of problems or implement certain types of solutions. Like a speaking engagement, the information should be high level and it shouldn't be a sales pitch. However, if done well, a solid white paper or eBook can be a great sales tool, not only for "cold" leads that visit your website or find you on Google but for warm leads who have been referred because of a specific problem that you address in your paper.

Note that white papers don't have to be long, only informative. 5-10 pages is plenty. If you are interested in doing a white paper but don't have the time to write it or lack confidence in your own writing, there are plenty of freelance writers out there who would be happy to help.

INSIDER'S TIP: Even if writing in long-form prose isn't your thing, you can still put out great content. Consider a tip sheet or helpful checklist as an alternative to a white paper. You may also think about putting together a solid presentation deck to keep things high-level and post for distribution on a tool like SlideShare. A really great presentation can sometimes be an even better tool than a white paper as it caters to the narrowing attention span of busy people in today's business environment.

Mesosphere: direct marketing to cold leads

If there's a chill in the air, it's for a good reason. We're a lot further from The Surface — and our comfort zone — than we've been before.

Marketing to warm leads is relatively easy. Send a steady,

but not overwhelming stream of messages to a friendly audience and make them feel good about doing business with you. And maybe putting together press releases, blogs, and presentations is hard work, but those initiatives also gave us credibility and, let's be honest, padded our egos a bit.

But now everything is about to change. Marketing to a stone cold and potentially hostile audience can be a deeply frustrating experience. But that's the nature of the beast when you're engaging in an activity that is likely to bring only about one positive result out of a couple hundred attempts. Essentially, you're looking for needles in a haystack.

Plus, direct marketing is also a lot more expensive than anything else we've considered at this point. Direct mail requires printing, addressing, and postage in addition to the purchase of a mailing list. Trade shows require airfare, hotel, show space, a booth, and marketing collateral — and that's just to do the bare minimum. Cold calling isn't itself expensive — you may have an unlimited calling plan and if you don't, you can get one. But hiring someone — even a temp or a contractor can be expensive.

So why engage in an activity that is so costly but gives so little in return?

Because these tools help you get your name out to a wider audience and put information about your company directly on the desk of your future customers with no middleman.

And, from an ROI perspective, you're going to do better with a direct marketing program than you will with any type of advertising initiative. Remember, in just about every direct marketing initiative you undertake, you will already know the names of your targets or — at the very least, their job titles and the company they work for — *a critical advantage over marketing via traditional advertising.*

By the way, you may be wondering why we mentioned trade shows in a discussion about direct marketing. If given the full marketing spectrum as presented in our chart earlier in the chapter, most marketers we know would have classified trade shows closer to The Surface, in the layer with PR. It's really a better fit here though and this is why:

All the initiatives we discussed in the previous layer — PR, blogging, white papers, public speaking, etc. — all build legitimacy and trust. If a news outlet publishes a story about you, it legitimizes what you're doing in a way that you can't do on your own. If someone reads your blog and appreciates the issues you talk about or learned a valuable tip when they saw you speak at last week's chamber event, you will earn their trust. Trade shows are not the same. You do not get any points on the trust scale simply by appearing there. Anyone who can afford to can exhibit in a trade show and the content of a trade show exhibition is generally sales-related and not about building credibility per se.

But similarly, these types of events are better than targeted advertising because you can look your audience in the eye, shake their hand, and make a pitch. Really, it's a lot like cold calling except in person.

Here are some tips on how to make the most of your direct marketing efforts regardless of the tools (phone, mail, or trade show) that you use to deliver your message:

1. As with all things, KEEP IT SIMPLE. If you try to tell someone everything about your business at once, they won't remember a bit of it. Start with a clear, concise, message and build the conversation over time.

2. Define your goals and stick to them. If you are using a cold call to try to win an opportunity for a live presentation, sell that. Don't make your whole pitch on the phone. If your postcard is designed to announce a new service, don't waste space trying to fit in references to all your other services.

3. Leverage the tools you created in the previous layers of your plan. If you're talking to someone on the phone or at a trade show and they mention a specific problem or issue, ask if it's okay for you to email them a couple of posts from your blog that address that specifically. If you have a white paper, leverage it in a direct mail campaign. If you get someone mildly interested, send them a case study that demonstrates success in a related field.

4. Do something memorable. In any of these initiatives, your goal is to interrupt someone's busy day and get them to notice you, listen to you, and think about you. That isn't easy and whitebread marketing is likely to yield less than stellar results.

5. Be *respectful of people's time* and expect to get very little the first time you make contact. If you send them a lengthy brochure with a lot of text, they likely won't read it. If you try to keep them on the phone or at your booth, they will become frustrated. Make the most of your short time by trying to move them to a venue like your website, blog, white paper, or to a meeting, or phone conference where you can have more of their attention.

6. Make the message as personal as possible. Obviously, you don't know these people, that's what makes them "cold." But that shouldn't stop you from adding some personalization to your campaign (which is not terribly expensive and often improves results). Incorporating a person's name, company name, and industry into a phone script or improvising elements of your trade show pitch based on cues from the person you're talking to.

7. In deciding whether or not to embark on a direct marketing campaign, make sure that you understand where your break-even point on the campaign is and how successful you have to be in order to meet it. If a campaign costs you $5,000 and you're mailing to 3,000 people but

your product is only $19.95, you're likely to break even. If your product is $1000 (and you have done a good job defining your mailing list), that may be a good risk.

8. Don't be wasteful. If you are going to spend the money, make sure you're spending it to reach your core audience. Don't spend the money on a big trade show if only a handful of people attending are likely to buy from you. Don't call or mail to every business or consumer in your home town if not all those people are right for you. Companies that sell mailing and phone lists will allow you to be VERY particular about who you include. You can include or exclude based on geography, income/revenue, industry, home ownership, size of business, etc. Be particular. A list full of poorly-qualified individuals or businesses will not make a successful campaign.

Direct marketing definitely carries risks and usually limited returns, but the benefits outweigh the risks if your strategy is executed well.

INSIDER'S TIP: A very important point — especially for businesses that sell to consumers — coupon envelopes/books and new home welcome packages are NOT direct marketing. They are advertising (just like newspapers and magazines). Just because something is delivered through the mail doesn't make it DIRECT mail.

A direct mail initiative is one where you control the entire piece and send it directly to someone whose name and address you have in your possession. In the coupon book scenario, you only control your contribution to the envelope or book. The firm you're working with controls everything else including the rest of the vendors allowed to participate and the mailing list. You should expect less response from that type of initiative than you would get by engaging in your own regular direct mail activities.

Thermosphere: targeted media

Make no mistake, this is advertising. But we need to give targeted media credit for being a lot less wasteful than mass advertising. In mass advertising, you put up a billboard or create a TV or radio commercial or newspaper or magazine ad and you as the advertiser have little or no control over who sees it.

For example, if we were to start a company that sold New York Yankees memorabilia, we could put a commercial on ESPN during SportsCenter and feel good that we're reaching sports fans. Targeted, right? Absolutely not. Millions of people watch ESPN and a majority are probably not Yankees fans. A decent percentage may not even like baseball. In this case, advertising on ESPN may be extremely wasteful.

Targeted media for this type of company would be Yankees fan club newsletters and magazines, Yankees fan websites and blogs, and any online or print outlets that focus on baseball memorabilia. If you felt for whatever reason that TV advertising was important, the Yankees-owned YES cable network, which airs primarily Yankees-related content would be a good option. In those venues, you are likely to reach lots of Yankees fans and relatively few people who don't care at all about the Yankees.

If you are absolutely compelled to advertise, use as much targeted media as possible and give preference to media where the results are measurable, the most popular option these days being Search Engine Marketing (SEM) where you pay not for the number of people that SEE your ad, but for each person that actually clicks through to your website or landing page.

Targeted online advertising can also work as long as you effectively manage your expectations and realize that your server won't suddenly be overwhelmed with traffic. Most online banner advertising — even to a targeted audience — doesn't bring more than a handful of clicks per thousand impressions. If you want those clicks to add up, you need to invest heavily in regular advertising.

Other examples of targeted media would be trade magazines, banners, or sponsorships on websites and blogs particular to your industry, sponsorships of events and associations that are important to your audience and sponsoring email newsletters sent by a third party to specific audience (for example, a baby food company sponsoring an email blast sent by a motherhood magazine to moms of children less than one year old).

As always though, use this as a complement to the lower layers of your marketing strategy and leverage the tools you've built there as much as you can.

Exosphere: mass media

Here's the honest truth: you should not advertise in mass media — newspapers, magazines, television, radio or billboards, unless you have the budget to support a regular and long-term campaign utilizing a mix of several mass media outlets and have no expectation of quick or measurable results.

Mass media advertising does have one major advantage over every other type of advertising and that is its ability to help boost awareness and recognition in the marketplace and to positively impact purchase intent over time.

But it won't sell your product for you and it is extremely wasteful in terms of its overall efficiency as a marketing tool for small businesses. This idea about "wasteful" has been mentioned before, so let us lay it out for you here:

Let's say you ran a high-end hair salon and took out an ad in your local newspaper or magazine to market it. Since you target women, and women are unlikely to listen to men about where they should go to get their hair done, half of the people reading the paper are suddenly useless to you. Now consider all of the other things that need to be right in order for a female reader to think about giving you a try:

- They need to believe that they can afford your service. A lot of local publications reach a wide range of income levels.

- Your location needs to be convenient.

- We don't know many women who never get their hair cut or styled. They are already going somewhere regularly for this service so there is an implied risk in switching hair stylists.

- Finally, they need to see your ad. Just because a newspaper or magazine is delivered to someone's home there is no guarantee that newspaper or magazine will ever be opened and even if it is opened and read cover to cover, there is no guarantee that your ad will catch their eye.

In the end, we are paying to reach a large number of people but will only connect with a small handful; and it should be clear to you by now that we could have reached those same people by spending less and following our marketing methodology here.

So if advertising is so awful why do all the big businesses do it? Advertising isn't awful, and we don't want anyone reading this chapter to walk away with that idea. There are many good reasons for big businesses to pursue mass media advertising but here are three:

1. From the big business perspective, although mass media advertising is somewhat wasteful, it is not all that inefficient when you consider the national and sometimes global campaigns that these firms have to execute. Consider the infrastructure that a large firm would need to build in order to market at the level that we recommend for small businesses. When you look at it that way, mass media suddenly seems cheap

2. Overall brand exposure, awareness and staying top of mind with consumers increases the value of big brands and increases the cost of entry for new competitors into their industry

3. In many cases, it's a cost of doing business at that level and it's something that's expected and encouraged by shareholders, stakeholders, and customers.

> If I was a buyer at a major grocery store, why would
> I give more shelf space to Coke if Pepsi was the only
> cola being advertised?

But these are rarely the concerns of small business owners and mass media advertising remains an effective way to get attention for your business. But it works much better as a cap on an already working marketing plan rather than a plan on its own. Use it when everything else is running like a well-oiled machine and if you believe that building more name recognition will help those existing marketing activities convert more leads into customers or convert them faster.

10 important tips to keep in mind as you're developing your marketing strategy

Some of the following tips may be summary at this point. As you sit down to figure out your marketing strategy however, these tips should help keep you focused and prevent you from going offtrack:

1. Get to know as much about your targets as possible

Reread what we said way back in the branding chapter about audience and remember that everything you do should mesh with their perspective, needs, and wants. Effective marketing is done FOR an audience, not TO an audience.

INSIDER'S TIP: "What's in it for me?" Every one of your prospects is asking themselves that key question whenever they make a purchase decision. Our job as marketers and business owners is to create tools and materials that help answer that question simply and emphatically. So whenever you go on a sales meeting or prepare your marketing collateral or website, make sure that you've given a lot of thought to the difference between the FEATURES and BENEFITS of your product or service.

This is actually a common mistake, and something that we talk about a lot to our clients. The problem starts with the gap between the seller and purchaser of any given product. As the people selling or marketing an item, we know it inside and out. We understand what it does and the things that make it unique and incredible. We innately know why everyone should want one. The customer, on the other hand is a stranger. They know little or nothing about us and often need our help to make good purchase decisions. We, on the sales and marketing side, are obsessed with features. They are often our differentiators and the things that we get excited about.

When Erik ran marketing communications for a global baby toy manufacturer, the company revolved around features. If they came up with a baby seat that played seven soothing songs while the competitor's product played only four, that was a good day in the office. After all, they were fighting a war for shelf space against larger, more mature companies like Fisher-Price. Anything that could provide extra ammunition when they went into battle was important. And seven songs is definitely more — and better — than four.

But what's in it for the end customer? Do they care how many songs it plays? Our customers, regardless of the industry, are obsessed with benefits. They want to know how their lives or businesses will improve by making this purchase. To the business owner, the benefit seems obvious because their extensive knowledge on the subject prevents them from being objective.

There's no doubt that features are important. But, they usually aren't meaningful unless connected with a benefit for your customers, which you can easily express in both conversation and collateral.

Before you do anything else, make sure you tell your customers what's in it for them. It may be the most productive change you ever make to your sales and marketing approach.

2. Don't jump the gun

Or, "don't try to run before you can walk." Don't spend money on an advertising campaign if you don't have sales and marketing processes or the right tools in place to help you close any potential business that comes as a result.

Build your marketing plan and toolkit strategically starting with the items that are most likely to help you CLOSE business and then build out to the items most likely to help you get prospects.

3. Your marketing toolkit is important. Build it right

This includes all your basic marketing tools and assets: your logo, your business cards, your company website, your PowerPoint presentation, your brochure, and other basic marketing collateral.

Hire a reputable firm to work on your these materials and be sure that you look hard for the right fit before making a commitment.

Again, don't do any aggressive outward marketing or advertising until you have these materials buttoned up. No use in drawing leads in when you don't have the means to make the professional statement that you'll need to close them.

4. Commit your plans and objectives to paper and keep them handy

Planning sessions are terrific. But their results don't ever really qualify as "a plan" until they are written down. But beyond showing the resolve to develop a strategy and commit it to paper, keeping a written plan serves other important purposes: reference and decision making.

Entrepreneurs constantly find themselves bombarded with new opportunities for advertising and promotion. So how do you decide which opportunities make sense and which do not? Consult your plan and see how these initiatives fit within your stated marketing objectives. A plan gives you an easy litmus test to use in your decision-making process.

INSIDER'S TIP: Erik has been telling this story for years and we're sure that just about everyone who's worked with him has heard it. Early in his career Erik worked as a designer and production manager for a network security firm and was always eager to impress the VP of Marketing with his boundless creativity. So he'd come into brainstorming meetings prepared to present his very best.

But his ideas very rarely made it onto the white board. Instead, his very best concepts usually got the following response:

"That's a great idea. For a different company."

Erik came to dread those eight words and he heard them often. But that experience taught him a very valuable lesson, which he has carried for years. We are all capable of having great ideas — MANY great ideas. But you can't implement them all. And most of your ideas, even some of your favorites — once taken into the context of your business — probably shouldn't even make it onto the white board.

Effective marketing, and effective overall business management requires a degree of moderation. You're always going to have more opportunities, more ideas and more creative insights than you will have the time, money, and personnel with which to implement them. So don't be afraid to kill the ones that don't fit straight off, no matter how creative or innovative they are.

5. Don't let your competitors make your business decisions for you

We all like to keep an eye on what the competition is doing; it's only natural and it's obviously a good idea. But there is no advantage to following them.

As we drool over that latest direct mail piece they put out and lust after that new packaged services deal they just introduced, we need to stop ourselves from the urge to raise our hands and say, "Me too!" When you let other firms in your industry be your proverbial shepherd, you compromise your individuality in the marketplace and lose credibility on claims of differentiation.

Be your own company and don't apologize for it. There are enough good ideas to be had out there that don't involve pilfering from your competition. And besides, who says that what those guys are doing is successful anyway? That new package deal may be unprofitable. That direct mail campaign, no matter how good it looked may have only generated two phone calls if any at all.

6. Beware of "too good to be true" advertising offers

Advertising doesn't work the way most small business owners expect it to. Entrepreneurs would love nothing more than to be able to write a check to a newspaper, radio station, magazine, or coupon mailer and sit back smiling as the phone starts ringing off the hook.

Unfortunately though, as we've discussed, this is an unlikely scenario and there is rarely a straight line between these types of "mass media" advertising initiatives and actual sales dollars.

So if a salesperson approaches you with an offer to grow your business by leaps and bounds simply by investing your marketing dollars in advertising with their firm, approach with caution. And, keep in mind that it is highly unlikely that any single marketing initiative will ever make a large impact on your business.

7. Don't try to do everything yourself. Find good vendors, partners, and advisors to help you

It's impossible for one person to do everything at once and unlikely that any single person possesses expert knowledge across every business function required to run their company. Just like professional baseball team managers have coaching staffs and the President has a cabinet, entrepreneurs need a team of people they can trust to help them succeed. Find people you can lean on and who will support you as you work to build your enterprise.

8. Don't hire a plumber to do an architect's job

"Marketing" has become one of the most overused and generic terms in the business lexicon. A lot of people will tell you they are in "marketing." In fact, they may be printers or sign makers, sellers of advertising, promotional products, or direct mail. These people may have an outstanding knowledge within their specialty and may be savvy and creative. But that doesn't mean you should trust them with your marketing strategy. You probably wouldn't want your plumber to design an addition to your home, nor would you allow your dentist to perform brain surgery.

Be careful of who you allow to advise you regarding your overall marketing strategy and be sure that it isn't someone who stands to profit from your continued patronage of one particular marketing tool over another.

9. Never lose focus on your referral business

It is easier, cheaper, and more profitable to sell to warm referrals (and existing clients) than it is to sell to strangers. You also have a much greater chance of success. So while selling to "cold" strangers may ultimately be a necessary marketing evil, make sure those initiatives aren't paid for with the time that you would have otherwise dedicated to earning referrals and additional business from existing clients. Other marketing work needs to be looked at "in addition to" and not "instead of" staying in front of your clients and warm leads.

10. Don't look for a single "silver bullet" solution

That one magic advertising buy that's going to fill your pipeline with eager, qualified prospects just isn't out there. Success in marketing takes time, patience, and stick-to-itiveness and just as the "get rich quick" schemes don't work in life, they don't work in marketing either.

This isn't meant to be an indictment of newspaper advertising, magazine advertising, coupon books, billboards, or any other flavors of mass media advertising out there. But as a small business owner, if you're going to use them, be sure that you're using them as part of a greater plan and not as a one-time "silver bullet" for quick success.

INSIDER'S TIP: Think about it: the same strategy + the same execution = the same results. Every time, guaranteed — it's just common sense.

So if you've been doing the same direct mail campaign for two years and interest has leveled off or started to wane, try something different. Refresh your message, offer, and graphics and see how it goes. At the very least you're giving yourself the opportunity for renewed success using a marketing tool that's started to get a little stale in your business.

If you have a website that you don't like because it doesn't look professional, have it redesigned. Then, celebrate by sending all of your customers, partners, vendors, friends, and family an email to announce your slick, new site.

Never get compliments on your business cards? Get a card that makes a real impact.

It's very easy for all of us to get caught up in the inertia of our business. We look at change as a costly, painful hassle. But very few of us consider the cost of staying the same. One of Erik's former corporate bosses liked to say, "If you do what you've always done, you'll get what you've always gotten." Truer words have never been spoken.

Chapter 4

Build a better website: the dos + don'ts

Web projects are challenging and always will be. Our team knows that just as well as anyone. In fact, we have no less than 15 web projects in various stages of completion as we write this. We know what to expect from the process and the technology, so we know what works and what doesn't.

We have also been around this block enough times to know that many small business owners do not have much experience — if any — in managing web design and development projects.

This chapter is meant to help you — the entrepreneur — get acclimated to the everchanging and sometimes counter-intuitive world of web design.

We're going to walk you through everything from planning, to your home page, to content, online video, and the bad ideas you should stay away from. In fact, let's start with those:

8 common small business web design pitfalls

Our "8 Pitfalls" represent some of the most common mistakes that we see business owners make during web design projects. Falling into any of these traps could lead to costly redesigns down the road or may even prevent your site from launching in the first place. Steering clear of these mistakes could save you thousands of dollars.

1. Poor planning + lack of overall strategy

This is the big one on the list. Your website is a business tool — just like any other in your company's arsenal and it needs to serve a function.

"But I just need a web presence as quickly as possible and I can't afford to do something strategic right now," the business owner says.

The truth is there's no good reason to push strategy to the

back burner. In fact, it costs about the same to have a reputable firm or designer build a great site as it does a lousy one. And over time, it costs much less to build a great site once you've factored in the costs of constantly redoing the lousy one.

When we tell people to take the time to think strategically, we're not talking about a process that will add months or years to the development cycle of your project. We're talking more like a couple of weeks. Sit down with your web group, your marketing advisor, or your business team and consider, "What function does my site need to serve?" Your website will likely have more than one purpose, but good answers would be lead generation, building credibility, generating e-commerce sales, increasing presence on search engines, or possibly even addressing an operational concern like an overloaded customer service team.

Documenting and understanding your business goals will give your design team great direction and will help them more effectively prioritize the elements in your layout. If your design group doesn't understand your business goals — or worse, doesn't care — you would be best served by firing them.

2. Flash abuse

This is a trap that a lot of business owners don't just fall into, but leap into — headfirst and blindfolded all while tossing fistfuls of cash into the wind behind them. Get the picture? A great many business owners want interactive, animated, Flash'ed-up sites because Flash'ed-up sites are, well, cool. It's a way that they can show the world and, maybe more importantly, their friends, family, and colleagues that they've arrived. But there's a problem: Most web audiences nowadays have a very LOW tolerance for Flash, at least in the way it's used in many sites.

For a vast majority of sites, Flash is best used as an accent — a means of doing something interesting, surprising, and unexpected with an element of your design. It's also useful in helping your home page "freshen" itself every few seconds so your audience doesn't get bored looking at it. But it's no longer considered okay to have people jump up and start talking to the visitor as soon as the page loads. Other no-nos are music or heavy video that start as soon as the page loads. And the once obligatory Flash "intro" is a complete waste of your money and your visitor's time.

Here are some basic dos and don'ts for incorporating Flash into your site:

DO: Animate your logo or another iconic element in a subtle and unexpected way.

DON'T: Use Flash in your navigation. This will cause problems with search engines and mobile browsers.

DO: Use Flash in place of an otherwise static and purely cosmetic image.

DON'T: Animate actual page content. This is bad for search engines and overall usability.

DO: Allow your users to play a streaming Flash video or audio presentation.

DON'T: Automatically start any audio or video upon page load. It's overbearing and, let's face it, annoying and potentially disruptive or embarrassing, especially when visitors surf your site at work or in a public place.

DO: Use Flash to accent your site. Much like hot sauce, a little goes a long way.

DON'T: Build all — or even close to a majority of your site — in Flash as this will likely cost you visitors and severely impact your site's presence on search engines as well as its "browsability" (if it wasn't a word before, it is now) on mobile devices.

DO: Use Flash to enhance your visitors' experience.

DON'T: Use Flash to enhance your ego or impress friends. Yes, this may be harsh, but so is the reality that selfish marketing NEVER works. But we see this time and time again with clients everywhere. This may not be the worst mistake you can make on the web, but it's arguably the most common.

3. Search engine negligence

We can no longer use ignorance as an excuse when it comes to search engines, so failing to acknowledge them when designing a site in this day and age constitutes negligence.

Now this isn't to say that all business owners should rely solely on Search Engine Optimization (SEO) best practices when scoping out a web project or even that every web site NEEDS to be optimized for search engines from the outset. But every site should be designed with search engine compatibility in mind so that SEO can be considered later should priorities change. That means using editable HTML text wherever possible/practical without hindering the design intent and minimizing the use of Flash.

There's really no good reason for an upstanding business owner to build a site that is difficult or impossible for search engines to index. This is a decision that everyone comes to regret sooner or later and this is a mistake that WILL force your hand in redesigning your site before it's time. Be sure to ask your web designer/developer how compatible your site will be with search engines while it's still in the design phases. If their answer is "not very," ask for some ways that you can remedy that and be sure to understand the trade-offs from a design perspective.

INSIDER'S TIP: Search Engine Optimization is a very fluid and ever-changing art. Just as Google is always making changes in their search algorithm, SEO experts must also constantly change or modify their practices.

But here's the real trick of it all: no one knows what the Google algorithm is and no one knows how they prioritize or weight the many variables there are in ranking a website. So what SEO experts consider "best practices" are really a series of educated guesses based on what they have seen have success in the past and what they have observed as they watch Google's behavior. If you are considering pursuing an SEO strategy, you need to make sure that A) you are prepared to make (or hire someone to make on your behalf) a neverending series of small tweaks and adjustments to the content of your website and that B) your site is built on a content management system so that it's easy to make those constant little changes. To quote Ron Popeil, there is no "set it and forget it" in SEO.

4. No calls to action

This is important, though a lot of entrepreneurs don't exactly know what it means. Here's an explanation: when you get someone to your home page, you need to lead them in a direction. You need to tell them what you want them to do now that they are there. Examples include:

- Sign up for a free consultation

- Get our white paper

- Buy our widget

- Join our newsletter

- Read our blog

- Learn about our new service

Don't be afraid to tell people where you want them to go and make it loud and clear.

Sometimes when we show a design concept that has a large call to action, the business owner will ask why we're drawing attention to something that is already available through the main navigation. Here's the answer: sites tend to have a lot of pages. Most small business websites (not counting e-commerce) tend to run from about 12 - 25 pages in our experience. All those pages are available in some fashion through the main navigation. But it's very likely that only two or three are REALLY important.

Use your home page and available space throughout the site to drive traffic to the important pages. Don't leave it up to chance that your audience will find that info on their own as they stumble through the rest of your site. When you tell people loud and clear how to get to the good content on your site, they will appreciate it. Their visit will be more productive if they can come to your home page and immediately find what they are looking for. Strong calls to action also increase the odds that a new visitor becomes profitable for you.

5. Looking inward for direction

All too often, we develop sites from our own point of view. We look inward at what WE selfishly want instead of thinking objectively about what our AUDIENCE wants.

Understanding what our customers and other stakeholders/constituents are looking for is a critical, early step towards success on the web. And, it has been a constantly recurring theme throughout this book.

If you don't know where to start, try creating a "persona" or a profile of your average customer. List out their wants and needs, their pain points, and reasons that they would — and would not — be inclined to do business with you (more detail on this is available in the branding chapter in case you missed it). Then create a different persona for each type of target customer that visits your website.

For example, if we had a products company that manufactured sporting goods, we would likely have one persona for an end consumer, one for a retail partner and potentially one for a school or private sports league if we sold through those channels. We may even want to create a media persona when outlining requirements for a news area or a job seeker for our careers section if those aspects of the business are key to our overall strategy.

Having these personas in our back pocket gives us an easy way to put ourselves in someone else's shoes. If we were sales consultants and identified that our typical client is a busy CEO who is short on time and wants to see fast results, we probably wouldn't want to make her sit through a lengthy video or online presentation. But we might allow her to request a specific day and time for a free phone consultation or possibly email some high level content that she can read at her leisure.

And here's another tip: "10 - 20 employee company in a service industry" is NOT a persona because it's not a "person." The office manager, CFO, or president at that company is though. Don't forget that only people can visit websites — companies cannot.

If you focus on addressing the wants and needs of your audience, it's a lot harder to take a wrong turn.

6. Using "If You Build It, They Will Come" in place of a marketing plan

Unfortunately, the "Field of Dreams" strategy rarely works in the real world. If it did, our job as marketers and web designers would be a lot easier than it is.

We tell a lot of our clients to think of their website as if it were a big event. You want people to come to your party, but how do you draw traffic? Odds are that reserving the ball room, DJ, and caterer won't be enough. You would start by inviting your friends and encouraging them to come. Then you might tell them to bring their friends and then you might think about ways to attract strangers.

Your website works the same way. If you don't do any work to draw people in, odds are that they won't come.

We've seen a lot of entrepreneurs look unhappily at their web stats and say, "What's wrong? We've got a great site and a great product, we've done the Search Engine Optimization. Where did we mess up?"

A client of ours contacted us last year with questions about SEO and why it wasn't working like it should. We looked at their analytics and found that nearly 75% of their site traffic was coming from search engines.

The first question that popped into our heads wasn't "Why isn't our SEO drawing enough visitors?" but "Why aren't WE drawing enough visitors?" There are really only four ways that someone can access your website:

1. Directly typing your URL or clicking from material that you sent them
2. Clicking a link to your website from another website
3. Finding you on a search engine
4. Paid advertising

In the case of our client, they only had three potential traffic sources since they do not advertise and one of those traffic sources was doing three times as much work as the other two combined.

Just think, if this company could just draw enough direct and referral visits to match what they were getting from search engines, their overall site traffic would increase by 50%!

And while retention programs aimed at current customers will help give the direct traffic numbers a boost, the biggest opportunity for success by far exists in building referral traffic from other sites.

Why? Because aside from the benefit of drawing the traffic from those other sites, those links will also create great SEO benefits. Popularity counts on Google and the more people talk about you, the more important you will appear and the higher you will get ranked and the more search-related traffic you will get.

And don't forget, if one of your competitors is consistently ranked highly by Google and the other search engines, it likely isn't by accident. It's because they worked hard over time, not only on their SEO, but also on their overall reputation and presence in the online marketplace. You can't expect to beat them overnight. But do the right things with your website and you'll get there as well. It won't be easy but it WILL be worthwhile.

INSIDER'S TIP: We all get those emails (almost always from people we don't know) promising a #1 ranking on Google and web traffic beyond our wildest dreams. All you need to do is pay. In our experience, there is no magic switch that will instantly put you on top of the heap at Google for only a few dollars. You can't "pay your way" to the top (except through pay-per-click search engine advertising) and success is very rarely instantaneous.

We consult with a lot of SEO experts in our business — we don't even try to pretend that we're experts at understanding how Google's search algorithms work. The SEO experts that are truly knowledgeable (and even they are making educated guesses) and can get results for their clients know that success does not come overnight. SEO is like getting in shape. You need to work at it constantly and reputable SEO experts are like personal trainers: they can help you meet your goal but ultimately, it's about persistence, patience and fresh content. Don't fall for the scammers who make these outrageous claims to make you #1 on Google tomorrow. It's just not going to happen.

The bottom line is that getting ranked highly on Google is HARD. If it were easy and if only a few dollars (or a few hundred for that matter) stood between any of us and a number one ranking, we'd ALL be number one. Again, stay far away from any claims of quick, EASY success on the search engines.

Remember what we said earlier about defining business goals online? Google's goal is to return the best, most qualified search results every time someone uses their site. And remember what we said about how Google is always changing the secret formula as to how those searches happen? They do that to ensure that their results remain pure and that they always stay one step ahead of the SEO guys who are always claiming they can crack the Google code. Google WANTS their engine to be as "SEO-proof" as possible and they have done a better job than anyone of maintaining the integrity of their search product over the years. Is the guy (or gal) who sent you that random, unsolicited email (and who likely doesn't even have a professional looking website) smarter than Google? Think long and hard about that before pulling out your checkbook. If it sounds too good to be true, it likely is.

7. Too Much Clutter!

Strange but true: it's very difficult to build a simple, elegant website. It takes a LOT of discipline and willpower on the part of the business owner. All too often, our instincts tell us to cram every bit of information we can onto a web page. This is not a winning strategy.

Oftentimes, web design is an exercise in restraint. It's easier to maintain boundaries in print materials; we are confined to the page. On the web though, many sites allow us to build pages of virtually infinite length, giving us room for as much text and as many photos as we could possibly want.

When in doubt though, keep it simple and, per pitfall number five on this list, always think of your audience.

Is your audience going to want to read all that text? Do they even have time? Will they understand what you're trying to illustrate in all of those images? Is this approach going to answer questions or cause confusion?

Assuming that a visit to your company's website is a step in the process of building a relationship with a prospective client, you don't need to give them ALL the details online. Give them enough that they can qualify your firm as a potential product/service provider and answer their questions by way of an email, phone call, or face-to-face meeting.

Trying to "jazz up" a simple but functional page with additional text and images just because you can is probably a misplaced effort and a poor use of time. Instead, we always try to go with the bare minimum of content necessary to make our point and inspire action from our audience.

We find that for the most part, the most successful sites are the ones that are friendly and approachable from the visitor's point of view. After all, these are the people we're trying to impress. If we overwhelm or intimidate them, they likely won't stick around for long.

8. Letting Small Functionality
Cause Big Delays in Going Live

This goes back to the first item on this list with regard to setting priorities. If your objective is to create a technological masterpiece or to use advanced web technology as a competitive advantage then obviously, the minor functional details can be tremendously important.

By contrast, if your objective is to promote your business and build credibility for your firm, the sophistication of your programming just isn't that important. And every day you allow your website to sit on the shelf because a little bell or whistle isn't quite ready does a disservice to your business.

If your car died would you go without a car for two months just because they didn't have one in stock with exactly the right sound system? Probably not. Most rational people would buy the car with the standard system as soon as possible and upgrade later.

Treat your website the same way, realizing that you only need four basic things to get "on the road" with a good site:

- A sound strategy

- A good resource for design and development

- Content

- A means for keeping the site up to date once it's live

All other interests with regard to a basic site design project are secondary and should be treated as such. You're always going to be better off with a live site that only does 95% of what you want it to than you will with no site at all.

Always be wary of the "show-stopper" when planning your web project. These are the little nuggets of functionality that will often become the most expensive part of the project and the biggest headache.

Keep your eyes on the big picture as much as possible and if relatively small functionality starts causing big problems, don't be afraid to table those items until after the launch.

The same goes for e-commerce. If you want to understand the complexity of your project should you require e-commerce, start by mapping out a traditional e-commerce purchase process:

1. Select category
2. Select product
3. Add product to shopping cart
4. Proceed to checkout or return to Step 1 to continue shopping
5. Enter personal information
6. Enter shipping details
7. Enter credit card details
8. Authorize credit card or, if declined, Return to Step 7
9. Transaction complete, merchant and purchaser notified

The more you deviate from these nine steps, the more custom work will be required which means a longer and more expensive project. And in many cases, those customizations may not bring in as much money as they cost to develop (a threshold you should be aware of as you are planning).

We usually recommend throwing out every custom feature that isn't absolutely necessary for doing business on a startup e-commerce site. If your business is new, your initial customer volume is not likely to be very high so you can afford to take certain parts of the process offline and handle them by email or fax instead in the short term. If your success depends on being able to sell direct via the Internet, get yourself in a position to be selling as soon as possible and keep your investment manageable.

Your early experience will probably also teach you things about your business and your customers that you did not expect and you will be thankful that you didn't overspend on frivolous functionality the first time around so that you can better direct your follow-up investment.

There always is a follow-up investment and your website will not last forever. You may as well plan for a "phased" build-out from the start rather than try to get everything and the kitchen sink in your site from day one.

Who wants "just" a website? Don't plan for mediocrity, plan for success

If we had a dime for every time someone told one of us, "I don't need anything special, just a website," we wouldn't be rich, but we could buy a pretty nice lunch somewhere. If you have a commitment to excellence in your business, that commitment needs to extend to your marketing materials and ESPECIALLY to your website. What makes the web different? Because upon hearing about you, meeting you, being referred to you, etc., the first thing someone will do is look you up on the web. Your website needs to make you look credible and trustworthy and something that looks "slapped together" just isn't going to cut it. Consider the opportunity you have to impress someone at that very moment, only to disappoint them terribly and leave them scratching their heads as to why you might be worth more of their valuable time.

A lot of times it seems that we as small business owners look at our marketing to-do list from a tactical rather than strategic perspective. It's a mistake that a lot of us make when we get so focused on getting things done. We forget why we're doing them and what we expected to get out of them in the first place.

There's no doubt that being tactical is easier. It's certainly less work for us as business owners and we are likely to get things crossed off our list quicker than we would if we meticulously planned and strategized around everything we do. But we're also more likely to come out the other end of that project with a "band-aid" type of solution that is not likely to get us the results we wanted long term. And soon we'll end up with another item on that growing to do list: "redo website."

It also goes without saying that most of us aren't marketing, branding, or web geniuses and can't sit down and come up with a brilliant, winning strategy in an afternoon. That's why the best recommendation we can make to someone who needs to start a new web project (but doesn't know where to start) is to contact an expert and ask for help.

Building a website is like building a house. You expect it to endure longer than your other marketing materials and starting from scratch carries a heavy expense both in time and money. If you build your site well the "chore" of periodically painting the rooms or rearranging the furniture is easy. But adding another room or moving the bathroom from downstairs to upstairs is hard. You can't expect that once your site is built that you'll be able to easily make it 10% wider, change the whole navigation scheme, or completely reallocate the real estate on your home page without incurring significant expense.

So the first thing we do when we sit down with a business owner and try to help them organize their site is understand exactly what the site goals are, what kind of audience we are marketing to, and what types of content we expect to have.

If our goal is sales via e-commerce, we're going to recommend ways to highlight products. If our goal is to build credibility, we're going to talk about how we can leverage blogs, video, papers, testimonials, and other content designed to make visitors feel confident about working with our client. The structure of your site needs to be defined by the business objectives you are looking to support.

Once we've discussed and documented those goals and defined our audience, we draw a site map to outline all navigation and all the content that will appear on the site. We try to keep things as simple as possible though the site map tends to expand about 20% once the client sees it and adds all the things that were forgotten the first time we talked.

Once you lay everything out, consider all your content very carefully (realizing that any item on your site map represents a page of content that you are actually going to have to write) and scratch out everything that isn't completely essential. Much as in our "8 pitfalls" discussion when we talked about how small functionality can keep your site on the shelf, so can little bits of missing content. If you are building your website on top of any kind of viable Content Management System (CMS), adding pages to an existing navigation structure should be very easy and straightforward. Make sure you're not trying to build a site that's bigger than what you're actually capable of populating with quality content.

INSIDER'S TIP: : If you aren't familiar with it already, the term "Content Management System" or "CMS" for short is likely to come up in conversation when you sit down with a web developer. A CMS is essentially a website behind your website where you can log in as an administrator and add/edit/delete your website's content. Should you have one for your site? Absolutely. If you do not have any HTML or CSS experience (or you don't even know what CSS stands for), without a CMS behind your website, you won't be able to make even the most basic website changes (correcting typos, adding a news item, or update an address or phone number) without contacting a professional.

If you are a small business owner and are operating under a tight web budget, don't spend your money keeping up with minor changes. If you have access to a CMS that's easy to use, you can do them yourself. Save your money for more significant online initiatives.

Here's the catch though: there are a million CMS solutions out there. Some are widely used, some are proprietary, some are very easy to learn, some are quite difficult. For a small website, we don't see any reason not to use one of the popular open source platforms (our personal favorite being WordPress. org). Some developers may want to lead you towards their proprietary system, but unless you have truly custom needs there is no reason to use a custom system to run a basic 10-20 page website.

If you go with the proprietary solution, you need to be resigned to the fact that you won't be able to hire another developer to modify it in the future. If something happens to that developer, their business or your relationship with them, you are stuck.

Have your developer pitch you their CMS du jour before you engage with them and ask for a demo of the editing capabilities. Also ask them how many of their clients successfully and regularly make their own edits.

With a solid CMS behind your site, you can launch with the bare minimum content required and then fill in the gaps over time.

Design vs. technology: which comes first on the web?

What comes first on the web? This is a question that we answer quite a bit and so we thought it might be helpful to answer it here. It's sort of the chicken and egg question: "What do I invest in first? Technology or design?"

The question itself implies that your budget is such that you can't achieve all you want in both of these areas at once, so you are forced to decide whether you want to invest your web budget on design or on programming.

There are a lot of programmers out there that are bound to disagree with us, but we always tell business owners to focus first on navigation and organization, second on design and overall experience and third on technology — the "bells and whistles" beyond the core functionality that you would just LOVE to see integrated into your company's web experience.

The purpose of technology on the web — and we're talking traditional corporate/marketing sites here, not community-based web 2.0 or social media sites where the form needs to follow function — is usually to enhance the experience of the site visitor and/or to enhance the site owner's ability to gather intelligence or solve operational inefficiencies. So if the overall organization of the site is poor and the site looks cheap or otherwise unappealing, the technology will never get a chance to truly shine. What's the point of having brilliant programming driving a site that no one understands how to navigate or that no one wants to look at? How will you ever streamline your organization by sending clients online to a site they will hate using?

It just doesn't work. On the other hand, a site that is organized well with your visitors' goals in mind will always yield positive results as will designing a great looking front end that projects the right image for your company. Do those things first and there will always be room for technology afterwards (that is beyond the bare minimum tech requirements: browser-compliant CSS/HTML and a

Content Management System you can handle). As the old saying goes, you only get one chance to make a good first impression — and on the web that first impression may only last a couple of seconds if you don't make good decisions when it comes to design.

What belongs on my home page?

A few years ago, it was easy to pick out the really cutting-edge websites. They were the ones with massive animation, music, sound effects, and a video that started running as soon as the page popped up. In fact, a "loading bar" was usually a sign to stick around because something cool was about to happen.

Now the web is much more mature and we're using it at a much higher level thanks to the proliferation of blogs, YouTube, Twitter, Facebook, Flickr, LinkedIn, and countless others. And, in our opinion, people are just not as impressed as they used to be with the "flashiness" of old. In fact, we believe that most of that nonsense has started to get in the way of our web experience rather than enhance it. Now the cutting edge websites are the ones that present the simplest and easiest on the outside and the most technologically advanced behind the scenes.

So how does this relate to marketing small business on the web? Flash and the obligatory "intro" movie have become passé and loading bars, once a status symbol, are now obstacles that separate your audience from the content they came to your site to find. Among our clients, we've found that the sites that are the most Flash/animation heavy tend to have higher bounce rates than the simple ones. The "bounce rate," by the way, is a measure of how many visitors come to your site and leave after seeing only one page. It could be coincidence, but everything else that we see happening in the marketplace tells us that this quick and unscientific study is a reflection of reality on the web today.

So what do you want on your home page? Slow-loading animation or video that scares your audience away? Or a simpler web design that encourages visitors to dig deeper? Many small business owners love the idea of having a flashy web site as they see it as a status symbol, a sign that they've made it. But we encourage entrepreneurs not to do it at the expense of earning business and opportunities online.

So what's going to make for a great home page? More than anything else, FOCUS is what's going to make your home page — and ultimately, your site — a success. The goal of your home page is to quickly qualify you as a product or service provider in your industry and give your visitors a clear call to action that shows them where they need to go next. Get more information, sign up, order, etc. The home page is also a good place to separate different types of visitors. A products company, for example, may need to separate consumers from retailers and present custom-tailored information for each or a services company may need to separate current from prospective clients.

Make sure that your home page has all of the following elements and everything else is purely cosmetic:

- Your logo, preferably in the upper left-hand corner

- A simple, easy-to-read navigation bar, generally below the logo and running either down the page or left-to-right across the page

- A visual focal point; it's important to make sure that you audience receives your most important message loud and clear

- A clear, concise call to action

- Cues that call secondary or tertiary audiences to more specialized areas of the site (i.e., a barbecue restaurant that also provides local catering services and ships their sauces and sides for home delivery nationwide)

- Enough text to support any SEO initiatives that you are pursuing

- A clear way for a visitor to get in touch with you if need be (could be a phone number in the upper right-hand corner or a prominent "contact us" link)

And that's it. As long as your home page fulfills these basic requirements, you can feel free to be as creative as you like provided that nothing else you do conflicts with one of these requirements.

INSIDER'S TIP: Draw a "wireframe" or blueprint of your home page, or better yet, have your web firm do one before any design work is done. This will give you and your web designers a means for organizing your thoughts and priorities before anyone gets too caught up in the excitement and anticipation that always comes with an initial design presentation.

What kind of navigation should I use?

At this point, there's very little that hasn't been tried on the web with regards to site navigation. This is one area where truly, you don't want to get too creative or too exotic. Your navigation should go across the top of the page or down the left. Your menu should NOT be built in flash no matter how cool it looks or behaves, primarily for SEO reasons (Google can not read content within a Flash movie and will therefore be unable to find the majority of the pages within your site without a navigation bar it can follow). In fact, we would recommend that your navigation be comprised only using plain HTML text, styled with CSS.

And don't let your designer push back and tell you there's no way they can be creative with that kind of limitation. Plenty of sites do it and do it well. The fact is, that approach is better for search engines, better for overall usability and better for you long-term when it comes to making updates and changes down the line.

INSIDER'S TIP: Don't ever let a creative person tell you that your design requirements — whether they stem from overall business objectives or SEO compliance — are "boxing them in" creatively. Obviously, we could all be creative if we had absolutely free reign, a blank check, and no deadlines. But that's not reality and to be a professional designer means being constantly challenged creatively along all of those parameters. Simply put, the best creative work in this business happens within boundaries. Find someone who isn't scared of that.

One navigation-related topic that has become a little controversial for us is whether or not to use a "drop-down" menu navigation on a site. In most cases we say, "No."

Why?

Here's the spiel: If the primary purpose of a site is marketing, the quality and success of your site as a marketing tool is going to be defined by your ability to tell your visitors a good story. You generally want people to see information or types of information in a specific order and lead them to a specific call to action like buy or call or email. Menu navigation severely impairs your ability to do that. When you expose the entire structure of the site from the home page, you invite people to jump around. They can get lost, they can get confused, and your story never gets told properly.

With a standard navigation scheme, you can lead people to the information they want. With a menu scheme, visitors are left to find it on their own. With a standard navigation scheme, visitors choose from a handful of links to click on. With a menu scheme, they can easy be overwhelmed by choices and intimidated by a site that looks much bigger than it is.

It's also important to note that contrary to the conventional wisdom that became popular in the late 90s, big sites are not necessarily better sites. If a good story can be told in five pages, what is the benefit of stretching it into 10? It comes from a selfish idea that a company's website will be somehow more significant or relevant the larger it is. That also combines with the financial interests of designers/developers/agencies who will obviously charge more to create additional pages. Consider how much simpler your site would be to manage at eight pages rather than 20. Consider how much more respectful it would be to your audience who can navigate your site in half the clicks and how much more effective your message would be if it were twice as accessible.

Our final argument against menu navigation is that a lot of people just don't like using it. It's too easy to "miss" with your mouse and lose the menu — not exactly the most user-friendly way to navigate.

So, for most sites, we strongly recommend against using the menu navigation. You'll find that you force yourself to build a MUCH stronger and well-organized site without leaning on your menu structure as a crutch. Your visitors will thank you.

Sometimes, just sometimes, getting a little lost is part of the experience. This strategy is popular among consumer brands that have a penchant for the unexpected. Brands that say, "I don't care if you find what you're looking for on my site, I just want you to experience it."

Chipotle has a long history of wackiness on the web. Their site is full of unexpected goodies on every page and includes a fair amount of complete nonsense like an

"Avocado Ripening Cam," a constantly-tapping pen, and a photo of their founder being hammered into place. Once you've seen a couple of pages, you're almost compelled to see them all, just to see what happens even if you don't care about the information on them.

But be careful about taking this kind of approach. Chipotle has hundreds of restaurants across the country along with billboards, radio ads, sponsorships, and more to help them establish that fun, tongue-in-cheek personality. Not to mention loyal fans that probably number in the millions. Small businesses don't have these kinds of luxuries. We can look at Chipotle's mildly confusing site and think it's cute because we know them pretty well. If the site's main purpose was to convince complete strangers to come in and eat, they may have gone in a different direction.

The written words: page content and white papers

We're not sure there's much that a small business owner actually enjoys about the web design and development process. But we are fairly certain that writing content is one of the most dreaded tasks of all, ranking right up there along with pulling out your wallet to pay your web firm's fees.

Unfortunately though, your site won't write itself. The first and best advice that we can give anyone about to embark on a project like this is just get started. You will procrastinate, you will make excuses, you will let your "go live" date start to slip. That is, unless you get serious about diving in. Be prepared to do whatever is necessary to focus, even if that means closing your door, shutting down your email, and turning off your phone to limit distractions. You may even need to stay up late or get up early a couple of times to get yourself into a good writing rhythm.

Bottom line: do what it takes and get it done. The longer you put it off, the longer the project will haunt you, and the longer your site sits on the shelf, doing nothing for your business and irritating your web developers.

Here are some tips to help you get it done and avoid biting off more work than you can handle:

Page content

As we discussed earlier, make sure that you examine your site map carefully and cross off any pages that are not completely necessary. There is no need to make your life extra miserable in the short term, especially when a good CMS will allow you to add those pages back in anytime, once the site is live and the pressure is off.

Don't feel compelled to turn every page into a short novel either. It usually doesn't take a lot of words to make your point and too much content will likely be intimidating and off-putting. Don't look at your site as a replacement for a full conversation and don't try to tell your site visitors absolutely EVERYTHING about what you do. Only give your audience as much information as they need to decide that you are worth talking to further. Once you are engaged in an active sales process, feel free to share as many of the nitty-gritty details as you like.

A nice page of content on the web is about two-to-three short paragraphs and a bullet list (if necessary). Strongly resist any urges to write more than that.

If, no matter what you do, you can't get your bearings as a writer, ask for help. There are a lot of fantastic writers out there who would love to work with you. Hiring a writer will drive up the price of launching your site, but as long as you can afford the luxury, that is a much better alternative to delaying weeks or months.

White papers

In case the term is unfamiliar to some readers, a "white paper" is a short document in which you, by way of your industry expertise, give advice on how your readers might address a specific problem in their businesses. White papers are typically not "salesy," and tend to take more of an advisory tone. The implication is that if the paper isn't enough to solve your audience's issue — *or if they need assistance in implementing a solution* — that you would be qualified to help them do so in a paid engagement.

Although white papers can be as long as 20-30 pages, they can also be extremely short. It's really the quality of your content that matters here, not the quantity. If you can tell a compelling story and relay some valuable information in just two pages, no need to write any more than that. Remember, you're not writing a thesis. You're writing something that needs to be useful for businesspeople and brevity may actually work in your favor.

If you're a business consultant and you think that having a paper would help add to your credibility, no need to write a dozen pages about how to succeed as a business owner — just write a couple of pages about failure points and call it "10 Reasons Small Businesses Fail" or something like that. Two pages still too much to write? Make it a checklist instead and let your audience self-assess their business woes. You aren't trying to capture lightening in a bottle when you do this kind of writing. Your only mission here is to demonstrate your knowledge and expertise in a non-sales venue.

White papers and similar content are obviously not required for a website. There is no need to pursue this kind of content if you don't believe that having it available on your website will help you acquire more new leads or help you close existing ones.

CONTROVERSIAL TOPIC: It has long been a convention for Internet marketers to recommend "trading" white paper (or similar) content for a visitor's email address using an online form: enter your information and you get a link to download the paper. Recently, we spoke to marketing expert David Meerman Scott who has a very different theory, counterintuitive to the industry standard approach. David suggested to us (and he details this theory in his book World Wide Rave) that white papers are more successful when there is no barrier to access.

Even though the paper is "free" on your site, you are still asking your visitors to pay by entering their email address and potentially by subjecting themselves to periodic sales pitches and emails from you. If there is no cost, David says that the readership of your paper will increase dramatically and the readers who are ultimately going to become good sales prospects for you will still self-identify as such even if you don't force them to provide their contact information before they download your content.

In the spirit of experimentation, we removed the email capture forms that come before all the white papers currently available for download on our site and in

the first month alone, we got more downloads than
in the four months prior combined. And we do not
believe that we lost any sales opportunities, though
that would be difficult to prove. There is no doubt
however, that a lot more people were introduced to
our company during our test month thanks to this
change in strategy.

To SEO or not to SEO?

We've been a little hard on the SEO guys in this chapter so
far. It's nothing personal, but unfortunately there are a lot of
guys out there who prey on a naïve small business audience
that just doesn't know what's true about success with search
engines. For every true expert we know, we've met about
10 who are less than honest with their customers about the
kinds of results they can realistically achieve.

There are obviously volumes of information out there about
SEO, but to help solve the knowledge gap in plain English,
we've written these 10 tips to help entrepreneurs speak
intelligently to SEO vendors.

1. There are many search engines out there and the number seems to be growing every month. But until further
   notice, only one search engine really matters and that's
   Google, which accounts for approximately two-thirds of
   all online searches. A lot of SEO guys like to talk about
   how many engines they are going to optimize you for

but there's no need to aggressively pursue anything BUT Google. And, according to most of the experts we talk to, what works for Google is likely to work for the other engines as well.

2. A lot of SEO guys will tell you how many search engines they're going to "submit" your site to. Google does accept submissions but some others do not. Even where these processes are available, though, submitting takes literally seconds and does not require any special access or credentials. Anyone can submit, including you. And by the way, search engines are pretty smart: they are likely to find your site even if you don't submit it anywhere. In our experience as soon as one prominent search engine finds a site, the others tend to grab it shortly thereafter.

3. The best way to improve your search results is to be mentioned on as many other trusted sites as possible. This is a signal to Google that people think you have good information and they will reward your popularity. Some SEO guys will tell you that they are going to create a "linking campaign" on your behalf that will address this, but tread carefully, as there is a lot of conflicting information out there as to what actually helps and what doesn't. If a trusted news source (CNN, Wall Street Journal, New York Times, Inc. Magazine, etc.) writes an article about you and includes a link to your site, that should help. We are also told that publishing press releases online us-

ing a distribution service like PRWeb is also a good idea. However, there seems to be some debate as to whether having your site included in a third party's "blogroll" or "link page" helps or not. Some experts we talk to say that Google recognizes this as a means to build links and does not count these. Keep in mind also that posting a comment on someone's blog with a link to your site included or posting your link on Twitter or a similar service also does not help. Sites like these use "no follow links," sort of a red light to stop Google from crawling them so their sites don't devolve into a means for SEO abuse.

4. Whenever we talk with someone who doesn't know much about SEO, they invariably mention "keywords" and "hidden tags" embedded in the document for SEO. What they are referring to are what web guys call "meta keywords" and "meta descriptions." According to just about every reputable SEO person we talk to, these tools — once central to SEO strategies in the late 90s and early 2000s — are now fairly useless. Some SEO people will still enter content there, if for no reason than to give Google more to read, but most reports suggest that while Google will read these tags, they are no longer factoring them significantly into their site ranking algorithm. You probably don't need to be too concerned with meta tags. What you should be concerned with is the content on your page and how often key words and phrases appear on your site. If you intend to be ranked highly for the

term "Atlanta import auto repair," that phrase should be included in your site content, page titles, etc. If it's not in your site's content, Google will never rank you for it.

5. Don't expect to be number one on Google, especially not for a broad term like "computer repair" or "graphic designer." If you want to make an impact, most SEO experts seem to agree that you'll get much further by targeting the niche or "long tail" types of phrases — the more specific the better. So, "Atlanta Apple computer repair" is a a lot better than "Apple computer repair." And "Buffalo, NY brochure graphic designer" is a lot better than just "graphic designer."

6. There are no guarantees of success and someone who makes you a #1 guarantee is probably blowing smoke. Expect to be in this for the long haul and expect that it will be a couple of months at least before you see any real measurable difference in your rankings.

7. Anything you can do, your competitors can do as well. You change your page titles? They can change theirs. You replace your site content with a lot of keyword-heavy text? They can do the same thing. If it sounds like an arms race, it is. If you are going to play in this space, it's probably best to prepare for a long battle with a lot of ups and downs, and no sustainable victory. You and your competitors are likely to change positions a lot.

8. If you want to absolutely guarantee being at the top of the page for any particular search phrase, consider pay-per-click advertising. As long as you are willing to spend money to keep that position and as long as you are prepared to outbid the competition (prices are set in an ongoing auction type of format) you can be number one. Just not in the "organic" results on the left. But it is immediate satisfaction and it may help you get the traffic you are looking for provided the cost isn't prohibitive.

9. If your business has an office or retail location, go ahead and list it in Google Maps. The process is easy and it gives you a chance of being listed in the "Local Results" that come up near the top of the page even if your site doesn't come up until page three in the regular results. If you work from a home office, you can still pursue a listing but be prepared that your home address will be public on Google for just about anyone to see.

10. Make sure you understand what you are going to get out of an SEO initiative. Set goals with your SEO professional along with a reasonable timeframe for evaluation. If you expect to increase site traffic 20% within four months, make sure you keep an eye on that. And if — after four months — you are no closer to reaching your goal, consider other ways to spend your marketing

dollars. Always be aware of the opportunity costs associated with maintaining an ongoing initiative like SEO.

So, you want to make an online video

By now, hopefully our position on Flash animation has sunk in: it's overused and fairly annoying if not done properly. But let's consider for a moment why Flash became so darn popular in the first place: back in the late 90s and early 2000s, it was tough to put video on your site. The files were large which presented a severe handicap in an age before broadband Internet was widely available in homes and small offices and even when you got the thing downloaded to your hard drive, you still had to open it in a separate movie player to view. Flash, however, allowed you to create motion graphics, which were relatively small in terms of file size and could be embedded directly into the browser window. Ten years ago, it was downright brilliant.

But now, the world has changed. Broadband Internet is everywhere: in coffee shops, sports bars, and even on airplanes. File size is no longer an issue. And thanks to new formats and the streaming video revolution, we can now play real video easily and reliably within a browser window.

We love online video: it's engaging, tells a story and — if it's done well — people will even be inclined to watch it.

We use it now on sites where we would have used Flash animation five years ago.

There's one thing that scares people when you mention video. It's the cost. So here's more good news: it doesn't have to be expensive and, thanks to the big amateur video movement online à la YouTube and others, it doesn't even need to be professionally done as long as it has a genuine feel.

If you do want to get something shot professionally, there are a lot of variables in video depending on what you actually want to accomplish, but your short video will cost anywhere from a few hundred to a few thousand. This depends largely on the experience of the production people you hire, the complexity of your shoot and whether or not you use professional acting talent or not.

Here are some tips for doing video right on a small budget:

- If you are on a small budget, say between $1,000 - $5,000, don't call a studio or a film/video production house. You're likely not going to get a call back for less than $8K - 10K. They'll never work within your budget. If you ever DO have the budget, don't hesitate for a minute to call one of those companies, they are absolutely worth it. And if a "professional video company" DOES say they can meet your budget, disqualify them immediately. Think local car commercials. Your best bet is to find a good freelancer. These are people that usually do a lot of work for the big production companies that you can't afford but cost a fraction of the price.

- Find free locations to shoot at: friend's houses, colleagues' offices, etc. We did a shoot in 2007 and got a great office location for free thanks to the generosity of the Johns Creek Chamber of Commerce. If you need to pay for permission to shoot somewhere, it is likely to cost you $1K - $2K.

- Hire young/inexperienced actors and don't go through an agency. They are looking to build portfolios and will likely do your video for free (or at least on the cheap) in order to get the experience and the credit. Don't know where to find actors? Try local acting schools or colleges that have acting programs. It's also possible that the people you hire to shoot your video will know someone. Note that free acting talent is a lot easier to swing when you are working on an "unsexy" B2B or industrial video rather than something for a consumer audience that will draw a wider appeal. And be upfront if you ever intend to use the piece as a commercial on TV. Actors will do a web video for little or nothing, but TV is, understandably, a different story. Don't "bait and switch" your talent.

- In non-critical/non-speaking parts, use friends/family/employees.

- There's lots of royalty-free music available at low cost on the Internet. If you happen to have a friend who's a musician, original music adds a LOT of production value to a video. The ability to get it free or cheap is too good an opportunity to pass up.

- Don't want to pay for the freelance videographer/editor? There are lots of student filmmakers out there who are talented and creative but, again, inexperienced. They may help you make a video for next to nothing plus the cost of renting professional equipment. If you go this route though, treat them like professionals — come with a clear vision and make them submit shot lists and storyboards so that you know you are going to get the product you want.

- If your video doesn't require any recorded live audio (i.e., it's just music and/or pre-recorded sound effects over video), you don't need professional equipment to shoot your video. High-end video is absolutely wasted on the Internet where everything is played at such a low resolution. So if the best you can do is your neighbor kid down the street who has aspirations of going to film school one day and a five-year old mini-DV camcorder, PERFECT! No one will ever know. But if you're recording live audio, it's a whole different story. You'll be sorry you used a consumer camcorder in that case.

- Budget up front for incidental expenses. Figure out what you need in props and any special wardrobe. Also make sure that you bring lots of snacks and drinks for everyone on the day of the shoot and plan on bringing in lunch for everyone as well. And then once you've set your this budget, increase it 15%.

If managing all this is a little scary and beyond your expertise, you can always hire an outsider to take care of everything for you. Doing so will add significant cost to your budget, but if you aren't comfortable playing producer, the cost will be low compared to starting from scratch if things get really botched along the way.

What if I have ABSOLUTELY no money?

No one wants to spend the several thousand dollars it will likely take to build you a winning web presence, but what if you just CAN'T spend the money? You don't have it, you won't have it for two more quarters, your credit cards are maxed out, you can't borrow it, etc.

If you're in this situation let's first answer the question that is likely running through your mind right now: "Can't I do without a site for the first few months or maybe the first year?"

While it's true that not every business needs a huge sexy site, every business DEFINITELY needs a web presence, even if it's only one page. You must have a URL to put on your business card and you must have a place where Google and Yahoo! users can find you.

The web is this century's yellow pages, shopping mall, newspaper, and knitting circle all rolled up into one. And because of the communal, ubiquitous nature of the web, none of us can really "opt-out" of it.

Consider all the people that could blog about you, "tweet" about you, post about you on epinions.com, review you on CitySearch, Kudzu, Yelp!, or any number of other community directory sites out there. And even if you only own a small, local business, customers can just as easily document their experience with you online as they can a big, national, or global business.

Do NOT give strangers the chance to control your brand online. This is a decision you are CERTAIN to regret.

By now, you should understand without a shadow of a doubt that a web presence is important and that you need one.

Without cash money at your disposal, the first avenue we would try to explore is bartering (or trading your product/ service to a web firm or designer in exchange for the site you want). This assumes, of course, that your product or service would be useful to someone in the web design and development business. But many times you'll find that a deal can be struck if you find the right firm. We do suggest strongly that if you do engage in a barter arrangement that you make it clear that you want to be treated as any other client, despite your unconventional payment structure and promise the same treatment to the other party. It's essential that the vendor/client relationship and the responsibilities that come with that remain intact.

If barter is not an option, our next best advice — before you spend $200 on a poorly made template that you'll never be able to use unless you already know HTML or $50 a month on an impossible online "site builder tool" — would be to get a free blog at WordPress.com and create a WordPress site to serve as your temporary home on the web.

We like this solution for a few reasons:

1. WordPress is easy to learn, easy to get your content in, and easy to get up and running in an afternoon. Really.

2. If you have never blogged before, a WordPress.com site will expose you to that and allow you to try your hand if you're interested.

3. When you are ready to replace this band-aid solution with a custom site (and you really should view this as a temporary solution), all the content, images, etc. that you have loaded in can be exported out and then imported into a site managed by the WordPress.org

CMS (note that WordPress.com is a hosted software-as-a-service platform, where the version available at WordPress.org is downloaded and then installed on your own web server).

As we mentioned earlier, the WordPress.org platform is a popular and highly customizable CMS that makes a perfect solution for most small business websites. The process for writing editing content is also nearly identical between the .com and .org versions so "graduating" to a WordPress.org site would not require any additional learning curve on your part.

Having a limited or non-existent budget is definitely a roadblock. But like all roadblocks, this is an issue that can be overcome, provided that you're willing to put in some time and effort. But don't let your budget (or lack thereof) beat you. You NEED to have a web presence for your business and don't use money as an excuse to try and ignore or neglect that need.

Chapter Five

Navigating the brave new world of social media

We are experiencing a seismic shift in the way we communicate, the likes of which we've not seen since email was first introduced. In looking back to the 1990s when email took off for both business and personal communication, it was revolutionary. The ability to send the same letter to dozens of recipients at once, to be able to forward someone else's email to another person, and the sheer speed at which all this took place was really cutting edge. Some predicted the demise of traditional mail while others forecasted that our reliance on electronic communication and other technology would further inhibit our interest in socializing and would increase "cocooning" (a term first coined by trend forecaster

Faith Popcorn in the 1990s) or social isolation.

To some extent, the Internet, mobile phones, and technology in general did have a negative impact on face-to-face interaction. Workers telecommuting from home, people renting movies without leaving their homes, online shopping, and teenagers communicating via text messages rather than voice calls all took their toll on personal interaction. It was easy to lose touch with people simply because they moved. A person's sphere of influence could vary wildly depending on where they were living, how long they had lived there, where they worked, if they attended a church, had kids in school, participated in volunteer activities, and so on.

Enter social networking. First there was SixDegrees. com, launched in 1997, which was one of the first manifestations of social networking similar to the format we see today. Next, in 2002, computer programmer Jonathan Abrams launched Friendster. In a manner of speaking, Friendster was the "original Facebook." Without going into why one has been more successful than the other, this was the beginning of the trend that has sent shockwaves through the advertising, public relations, and media world. Most notably, in June 2009, Twitter was historically entwined with the election results and ensuing violence in Iran that elevated the service to an almost hero status because it was the only site that the government was unable to block. Some news media were even referring to the situation in Iran as the "Twitter Revolution." How's that for boosting your company's valuation?

Social networking seemed to appear at just the right time. Just as we had become more isolated through technology, another technology stepped in to save us from the original technology. Sound confusing? Perhaps we could loosely apply Newton's Third Law: For every action, there is an equal and opposite reaction. Humans are inherently social beings so the natural reaction to our increasing social isolation had to be something that counteracted the force that was driving the virtual wedge between us. Since 2002, there has been an explosion of these social networking sites that have not only re-energized the internet — what many are calling Web 2.0 — but reconnected us to people in ways that traditional forms of communication previously could not.

Our sphere of influence is no longer dictated by distance or time. We can reconnect with people from our childhood or connect with new people through our past and present connections. And, while we don't actively communicate with these people by sending them messages directly, we are aware of their presence. And, when necessary, we know how to reach them. Writer Clive Thompson refers to this "ambient awareness," a term coined by social scientists in his September 5, 2008 New York Times Magazine article:

"Social scientists have a name for this sort of incessant online contact. They call it 'ambient awareness.' It is, they say, very much like being physically near someone and picking up on his mood through the little things he does — body language, sighs, stray comments — out of the corner of your eye."

You may not care enough to respond to the fact that someone's cat just died or that their child lost his first tooth which you see via a person's "status updates." But, you have an awareness of what is happening to the people in your virtual sphere so that if and when you do see them in person, you can have a more meaningful interaction because the need for small talk has been taken care of by this "ambient awareness" you now have of that person. And, because of the digital intimacy you have with someone, you are more likely to take note of a recommendation from this person about a product or service experience they may have had.

So, what is the relevance of the social media revolution for small business? As we discussed previously, many small business owners say that their best customers are referrals from other customers. Before the advent of social media, that might mean that your happy and satisfied customer would tell a handful of people about your product or service. However, in the age of social networking, your one customer may tell hundreds — if not thousands — of people how much they like your product or service depending on what social media platform they are using to get that word out.

As a business owner, your ability to tap into this cavalcade of information could be the difference between your success and failure. In addition to having your customers out there spreading the good word about your company, you have the unique opportunity to engage in conversations with both your current and prospective customers. There are many examples of companies who are doing this correctly but the shining example has to be Zappos, an online retailer that primarily sells shoes. Run by CEO Tony Hsieh, the company employs social media to reach out to its customers and also encourages employees to utilize social networking to build morale and camaraderie within the company.

Twitter is actually part of Zappos's corporate training. Zappos has done a phenomenal job of building a very open and trusting company that empowers employees to provide the best customer service depending on the situation. If an employee believes that flowers need to be sent to a customer to thank them for ordering from Zappos, they can do that. That customer may then go on to broadcast that user experience out to their social network creating more positive "press" for Zappos.

Just as humans are inherently social, they are also inherently distrustful of information that is spewed at them through mass media. Nonetheless, traditional advertising, infomercials, direct mail, and print ads still have their place although for a small business owner, these approaches may not be an effective use of their marketing budget. This is because traditional avenues rely on repetition, repetition, repetition — which costs big bucks. Therefore, capitalizing on social networking as a business tool is both smart and necessary for small business.

Where do I start?

If you look at the number of social media sites on the Internet, it can be a little intimidating. Certainly, there are the big hitters like Facebook, Twitter, YouTube, LinkedIn, and MySpace. But, that's just scratching the surface. There are multiple blogging platforms such as Blogger, WordPress, TypePad, and Tumblr just to name a few. It can be overwhelming given the seemingly infinite number of choices in each category from social networking, blogging, to video or photo sharing, social bookmarking, and more. But, before you go and sign up for every single service out there, take a moment to think about your overall objective. There is no "one size fits all" approach because each business is different and the way it will communicate with customers must be tailored to fit their audience.

We recommend that you consider your audience and then pursue no more than TWO of these tools at once. You can always expand your campaign over time, but getting overwhelmed in the first week is a sure path to failure. Focus your attention on really learning one thing at a time and don't allow yourself to become distracted with other sites.

INSIDER'S TIP: It seems like everywhere you turn these days, someone is hanging out a shingle and calling themselves a "social media expert." The truth is, it's not rocket science. Someone saying they are a social media expert is like someone saying they are an expert at using a fax machine or the telephone. It's simply a new way to communicate.

In fact, in April, 2009, Marketing Sherpa published an alarming statistic. It seems that 2/3 of marketers working in organizations that "have not used any form of social media marketing or PR" self-identify as experts in social media. How is this possible? Are they learning by osmosis? Do they have friends that use social media? Or perhaps they've just been reading and watching the increasingly frequent news reports about social media.

It's obvious what's happening here — Sherpa drew the same conclusion — companies and organizations are feeling pressured to dive into the Social Mediasphere and tapping the person in their group who has the most friends on Facebook or maybe a semi-complete LinkedIn profile to become their social media maven. That's fine and it's only natural that firms try to develop these initiatives internally. It is also clear by the ever-increasing number of "social media experts" popping up on the web — and everywhere else for that matter — that a good number of marketing, PR, and web professionals are seeing dollar signs in "social media consulting." But that these people should automatically consider themselves an expert is ludicrous.

Want to know how to become an expert? USE the tools. Use them extensively for a period of months and figure out what works for you and how you can become successful — or not — using online networking.

After all, the social media community doesn't need another self-proclaimed expert. It needs people who are actually willing to contribute to the conversation in an open, meaningful, and HONEST way.

So, be careful not to be taken by someone offering to get you 10,000 followers in 10 days for the low, low price of $199.99. That's not how we recommend using the social networking tools we discuss in this chapter.

Twitter (www.twitter.com)

First off, get over the fact that it's called Twitter. You're not going to turn into a "twit" because you use it. It could be called anything and it would still be just as useful. Why? Because Twitter can be used in many different ways. One of the first ways we recommend using it is as a listening tool.

If you own an established company, you might log on to search.twitter.com, type in your company or product name and find out if people are talking about you. If not, you have an opportunity to "start the conversation" so to speak. If they are talking about you, you will most likely come across at least a few negative comments. You can't please everyone. But, the good news is that you still have the opportunity to join that conversation and potentially correct any problems — real or imagined. Also listen to — or "follow" as it's called on Twitter — people in your industry or people in business who you respect. You can learn a lot just by following successful people. In this way, you are using Twitter like a personalized newsfeed.

If you are starting from scratch and no one knows that you sell purple widgets, you will have the opportunity to introduce your product to the Twitterverse. Twitter is often described as a "microblogging" tool which is yet another way to use Twitter. Since you can only tweet 140 characters, you cannot be as wordy as you can on a normal blog. So, if you are pushing information out about your product/

service, you have to keep it short and sweet. You can always reference a blog post or link to a picture of your product using Twitpic or yfrog. The point is, what you put on Twitter has to be very succinct. There's a bit of an art to writing short posts so you learn by using it. Remember, too, that all your messages are public unless you use the Direct Message feature, which is similar to a short email.

Facebook (www.facebook.com)

Since Facebook began as a service for college students, it has retained some of its youthful image as a site for the 30 and under crowd. However, that is quickly changing. With over 200 million subscribers, Facebook is on its way to becoming as main stream as it gets. According to Nielsen Online more women are using Facebook and many make over $60,000 per year. Grandparents are on Facebook now so they can see what their children and grandchildren are doing.

Facebook is rich with features that give users the opportunity to display snippets about their lives and share pictures, the events they may be attending, and what people, products, or services they consider themselves "fans" of. Fan pages can be created by actual fans or they can be created by the company itself. Either way, the goal is to connect people who like a certain product to each other and to the company that makes that product. You can then choose to advertise your page if you want to pay Facebook to target a certain demographic (physical location, gender, age, etc). If you have a website, make sure to put the link to your Facebook Fan Page there as well as any other social media profiles you have created. You can also reward people for becoming a fan with a coupon or small free gift with their next order. The possibilities are endless.

That said, Facebook may not work with every product or service so be sure to understand your demographic before you going to the trouble of creating a page.

Blogs

At this point, it's probably useful to a discuss how a blog might help your small business. We're going to take a leap of faith and assume you know what a blog is but what you may not know is how to use it effectively. If you don't have a website yet, a blog is a great way to establish a "home" on the internet.

INSIDER'S TIP: If you can't yet afford to have a website built, purchase your .com domain name from GoDaddy and forward it to your blog. That way, you will have the domain name once you have the funds to pay for a professionally-built website. Your blog can be transferred to your site so you won't lose all your valuable content.

There are several popular blogging platforms available: WordPress (.org or .com), Blogger, Typepad, Moveable Type, and Tumblr. Most of these are free or very affordable options in terms of creating an online presence. This is especially true if you don't already have a website. They are very user-friendly so you don't need to understand HTML or know how to code to create a relatively good-looking site. Most use templates so your blog may look like thousands of others out there but at least the content will be original.

Content is really the key when it comes to blogging. Whether you are using a free service or hosting the blog on your custom-built website, what you say and how often you say it will determine the number of regular visitors you might have. Creating and maintaining a blog is hard work, however, so be sure you are prepared to make the time commitment required to keep it current with fresh, original content. There's nothing worse than clicking on a company's stale blog that hasn't been updated in months so don't even bother starting one unless you are prepared to go the distance with it. But, if you are committed, a blog can be a great tool for small business because:

- It establishes that you have more than just a cursory understanding about your industry. You have the opportunity to showcase your expertise about not only your product or service but about your industry as a whole. People are more likely to trust you if they feel like you are staying on the cutting edge or keeping up with trends in the marketplace.

• It creates a community of followers where fans of your company can come to find out the latest news about what your company is doing or what is happening in the industry. Having a comment section further enables the interaction between your customers and your company and between customers themselves.

• Unlike your website which may remain fairly static, a blog keeps your site updated with fresh content making it more "SEO-friendly."

INSIDER'S TIP: As we discussed in the Web chapter, SEO (Search Engine Optimization) is an inexact science at best because unless you work for Google, you have no idea how they, or any other search engine, determine which sites rank in the top 10. However, it is widely known that having fresh content on your website in the form of a blog can greatly increase your chances of being found by a search engine.

LinkedIn (www.linkedin.com)

LinkedIn is like the professional version of Facebook. You can connect with people you've worked with or help someone else connect with one of your contacts. It is a home for your online resume. Your contacts can see where you have worked, what your area of expertise is and perhaps refer potential customers to you. Recently, LinkedIn has added the ability for users to connect their blogs, Slideshare presentations, and other third-party applications to their profiles. This helps to cross-reference your company's online presence.

Sean Nelson, author of The LinkedIn MBA and two other books on LinkedIn, explains that your LinkedIn profile not only needs to be complete (i.e. clear photo, good tagline, and fully complete professional history), but you also need to be clear about why you are on LinkedIn. He thinks that you should be on LinkedIn as a way to make money. Of course, to do that, you need to have a network of people. One of the best ways he believes you can do this is through the Groups feature. Because, while you may have direct connections with perhaps 2,000 people, you can potentially reach hundreds of thousands of people through your participation in the various groups.

The other important thing Sean believes you need to do is build credibility. People have to trust you in order to want to do business with you. One feature that LinkedIn offers is something called Answers. Relying on volunteers in LinkedIn to answer questions from other users, this is a great way for you or your company to get some exposure and further position yourself as an "expert" in your field. As long as you are answering the questions objectively and not doing too much self-promotion, you will appear more credible and if someone would like to find out more about you, they can visit your profile.

LinkedIn is also a great way to search for potential employees for your company. Many recruiters rely on LinkedIn for their candidates. So, take advantage of the fact that this free service is there for you to connect with other talented people in your field.

INSIDER'S TIP: Once your profile is 100% complete, make sure your LinkedIn profile is public. Assuming you haven't shared too much personal information, you should do this because if someone "Googles" your name, your LinkedIn profile is fairly likely to show up near the top.

YouTube (www.youtube.com)

If you aren't keen on the concept of a blog or you simply don't want to write something everyday, consider a YouTube Channel. You could create video posts, which feed into your blog or in this case vlog (Video Blog). This is a little trickier than writing a blog post because now you have added the additional elements of sight and sound to your online presence. If you are not a good public speaker, then perhaps consider hiring a spokesperson to create your video content. And, this should go without saying, but make sure that the quality is good — audio, video, lighting, and the way it is edited. It should be clear and concise.

One of our favorite examples of a company that successfully used YouTube to generate buzz about its products is Blendtec. Blendtec makes among other things, blenders. It has its normal, everyday demonstration videos on the corporate website at www.blendtec.com which we're sure a few people watch. But, in a campaign that can only be described as **pure genius**, founder Tom Dickson appears in a series of retro-looking video infomercials called "Will It Blend?" to showcase the power of his blender. In them, he attempts to blend things such as cameras, iPods, golf balls, glow sticks, marbles, and cell phones. Each video comes with the "Don't try this at home!" warning clearly stated. Dickson appears on camera wearing safety goggles, gloves, and a white lab coat and always asks the question, "Will it blend?" at the start of the video. His charming and nostalgic demeanor — reminiscent of an advertisement from another era — coupled with the unconventional items he places in the blender make for an entertaining campaign that has had the effect of boosting sales for the company. At last count, Blendtec has 196,071 subscribers on YouTube and its channel has been viewed 3,754,907 times. There is also a spinoff corporate site called "Will It Blend?" located at www.willitblend.com.

You may not be able to create the next "Will It Blend?" campaign, (which is really an extreme example of how a company's advertising can go "viral") but if your content is helpful and informative, you are likely to get some subscribers and potential customers through this medium.

Reaching local customers

One of our local restaurant groups here in Atlanta decided to begin a social media campaign as an experiment. About two years ago, Fifth Group Restaurants began on YouTube with posts of several short clips of their employees discussing why they enjoyed working for the Company. This worked as an excellent HR tool to give potential candidates an "insider's" look at the corporate culture according to Michael Erickson, Director of Marketing for Fifth Group. From there they branched out to other forms of social media including Facebook and Twitter. Michael said that since establishing their Facebook presence a little over a year ago that it has grown tremendously. Each restaurant and executive chef now have their own fan pages that are used primarily for guest feedback and event postings.

At this printing, they've been using Twitter for the past six months. It's the most recent addition to their social marketing efforts and it's working well to help connect with their guests.

We asked Michael for an example of a success they experienced using social media.

"We posted a secret password to Twitter and Facebook that, when used in the restaurant, rewarded the guest with something complimentary, i.e. a drink or appetizer. Considering it cost us nothing upfront, the return was excellent," said Michael.

Michael says that he spends about an hour a day posting, reading or responding to social media on Yelp, Facebook, Twitter, and myriad of blogs. "Social media plays a critical role in our marketing because it allows us another real-time touch point with our guests. It extends the dining experience beyond our four walls and into their homes, offices, and mobile phones — all at minimal cost. The full potential is exciting and unrealized at this point and we're really enjoying learning about how it can further enhance the guest relationship and experience in a positive direction."

What kind of ROI is in social media?

Clients are shocked at our answer when they ask what their return on investment (ROI) should be from using social media tools. Our answer? It depends. There is no standard yet on what an acceptable metric is for measuring the impact of a social media program and the medium is, frankly, still too young to have widely accepted best practices. It just isn't easy (and oftentimes impractical) to assign a percentage or dollar figure to your efforts, especially if you have never had an active social media strategy.

We recommend setting objectives for your program and then kick off a trial period of three months or more where you monitor your progress, tweak your approach and see how modifications in your strategy affect the outcome. Then you can use your data to more accurately predict a long term return. This can be problematic if you need to secure a budget from upper management, but small businesses are less likely to face these obstacles. Remember also when discussing ROI that social media marketing is cheap: the tools are free and anyone with basic computer skills can participate. Your monetary investment is likely to be next to nothing; your time investment is what really counts.

As with any intiative, there are both qualitative and quantitative ways to look at your efforts in social media.

Qualitative

Before beginning, ask the following questions:

- Is our company currently engaged in the "conversation" that is happening about our products or industry?

- What are people saying about us or our competition?

Once you or your company has fully engaged with an audience via a variety of social media platforms, then ask:

- What types of relationships are we building with current and potential customers?

- Are we now part of conversations that we weren't previously?

While not an exact science, you will find that you can answer these questions with a fair amount of accuracy and at least determine if your efforts have been successful.

Quantitative

Certainly there are ways to measure an uptick in sales that may (or may not) be the result of a company's social media efforts, but to try and directly correlate them to social media participation may be difficult. Instead, use tools such as Google Analytics to measure site traffic or Feedburner to determine how many subscribers you have on your blog. If your business is e-commerce based, be sure to also carefully track changes in sales patterns and conversion rates. In any event, whatever methodology you choose to "measure" your results, understand that you may be guessing at the impact your social media presence has had on your business. This is especially true if you are still utilizing more traditional marketing and public relations initiatives.

As we stated before, anyone can proclaim to be a "social media expert" and certainly there's a lot of that going on these days. We don't know many true experts in this field so if you are still confused and believe that you cannot possibly do this on your own, it's probably best to consult a company that offers social media services in conjunction with traditional marketing initiatives. Putting all your eggs in the "social media basket" doesn't make sense anyway. If you have the budget, greater importance should be placed on building a professional brand and online presence. The social networking can complement your traditional efforts but they will never supplant them.

Controversial Topic: is quality or quantity most important when building my social network?

This is a big topic of debate amongst social media users. Is it better to be connected with a LOT of people or relatively few, provided that those people are of an especially high caliber?

We usually fall on the side of quality over quantity, though there is sort of a "practical minimum" number of connections that you should seek to maintain. On LinkedIn, you should certainly have enough to qualify for a 100% complete profile. On Twitter, serious users will almost always have a few hundred followers at least. Once you have attained these minimum levels, we honestly see no reason to collect people online as if they were baseball cards.

Others, however, see power in numbers and, depending on how you intend to use these tools, there may be merit to the argument.

Scott Allen, who has been on our radio show a couple of times, is a true social media expert and — as we have affectionately nicknamed him — the Nostradamus of the Social Media Age. Scott actually foretold the emergence of social media in his book The Virtual Handshake which was originally published as an eBook in 2003 and officially hit bookshelves in the summer of 2005. Scott told us once that he considers himself like "the first guy who decided to be an auto mechanic when 95% of the world was still driving horse and buggies."

Scott surprised us when he came out strongly in favor of the "quantity" argument in talking about how he decided to build his Twitter following. Since he can explain his thinking process better than we can, a partial transcript of his appearance on Gravity Free Radio on July 14, 2009 (the full interview is available for download via podcast at gravityfreeradio.com/scottallen) is below. Note that although he has decided that it is important — for a variety of reasons — to maintain a very large Twitter following for himself, he also discusses the challenges it presents and says very clearly that having a lot of followers does not make him more of an expert, nor does it make him more credible. He had something else in mind when he began aggressively trying to increase his follower count:

Erik Wolf: *You said something interesting on Twitter a couple of weeks ago. You said, "I've come to the conclusion." I'm now paraphrasing, but you said, "I've come to the conclusion that I need more Twitter followers. I need a lot of Twitter followers." Explain that. Please share what your thinking there was and where you see the benefits.*

Scott Allen: *A little quick context for that is that I am known as a social media consultant. I have particularly been in the business-to-business space and have emphasized everything about authenticity and transparency and having conversations and all of that good stuff. I still absolutely feel that way. Here is the thing, Twitter is an interesting communications tool. That is what it is. Twitter is not a community, Twitter is a communications tool. It can be used for one-to-one messaging and private conversations, it can be used to have a conversation with one person and have a few people listening on it. It is also a broadcast medium. It is all of these things depending upon how you try to use it.*

There are a few things I discovered. Basically, what really drove this for me is that I have been mostly involved in the business-to-business arena and I got involved with a business-to-consumer project and kind of tried to do a soft launch to see what response was off of my own personal network, which at the time was 4,300 people, all achieved "organically." My response rate was, in a word "disappointing." In terms of the response I got on Twitter to my announcement about this. So I went to a couple of my friends who had much, much larger following accounts, on order of magnitude, like 10 times as many followers as I did, they have added them through proactive following techniques. Proactive — you follow people and they follow back. What happened was that I found out that as a percentage response rate, their percentage response was about half what mine was. Half. Their total follower account was 10 times, net result five times better raw responses.

Erik Wolf: *Which follows the study that Mashable just published about the response rates to Twitter announcements based on follower counts. They talk so much about the fact that your percentage goes way, way down but of course you have so many more people that you are talking to that the response is still better.*

Scott Allen: *Bingo! That is just counting the first wave response. When you multiple, when you take that out to two to three degrees of separation with re-Tweets, it ended up actually being significantly higher than that. Because the five times better rate at the first level but a 25 times better response rate at the second level. It actually ended up being about 12. So, the point* *is that if I wanted to use this as a channel for promoting a broad business to consumer kind of thing, if I want to work those into my conversation then I needed to do that.*

Basically, the celebrities have arrived at Twitter. Nine months ago you could be on the front page of Twitterholic, which tracks the most followed people on Twitter with under 100,000 followers. Now, you'll be somewhere in the 300-400s if you have that many followers. Twitter's own behavior is promoting that... When you join Twitter, they say here are some suggested followers, Ashton Kutcher, CNN Breaking News, The Real Shaq, MC Hammer. So, Twitter is, sort of, the worst offender at doing this, at creating these Twitter celebrities.

There are also a lot of tools out there that figure your Twitter follower count as part of an overall score, like Twitter Grader. There are also several authority based Twitter search tools. The fact of the matter is that if you have a higher follower count, you are going to present higher in these things. I don't care a thing about my follower count for its own sake. I am not trying to brag about my follower account. I am not trying to say that I have 27,000 followers makes me more authoritative than someone with 270.

Erik Wolf: *I'm impressed you are still talking to me, Scott!*

Scott Allen: *(laughing) What I am saying is the reality that the way that the Twitterverse has evolved is that if you want to use it for any kind of mass media, for any kind of larger, broader audience then go ahead and do so. The thing is it doesn't preclude* *you being conversational. That is the mistake a lot of people make. I still follow the same guidelines that most of the social media people are saying, that only 1/20 of your Tweets should be overtly self-promotional. I have conversations one-on-one with people and I reply to direct messages that are truly directed at me. I reply to conversations and everything else. I still use it in the same way. I do have to use some filters, because I obviously can't read a stream of 25,000 people and everything they post. So I have sort of funnels. I have the social media people who I follow. I have the Austin people I follow, I try to keep up with people locally. I have my VIP group of about 30 people who I count as close friends, who I really want to see and make sure I see everything they have to say. I use tools, I use TweetDeck to help filter those out. Every once in awhile I take a dip in the big stream and anyone with half a brain knows that if I am following 25,000 I am not reading every single thing that they write…*

You manage your attention. I am sitting here spending half an hour on the phone with you. I can't spend half hour on the phone with everybody I know. How often could I do that? We are selective about how much time and how much attention we spend with people, depending upon how well we know them. All I am doing is letting Twitter, instead of being a little small box, I am using some tools to give me those little small boxes and a lighter attention at the broader level. The people who like what I have to say, they end up moving down the funnel.

Case in point, the very first day that I bit the bullet and said, "Alright, I am going to go on this high-following scheme." The very first day I did that I focused on people in Austin and I followed 1,000 people in Austin in one day. I kicked it off in the morning. I read all the direct messages I get back. A lot of them are junk, cause they are auto-welcome messages that are spam. But one person said, "Hey, great to meet another Austinite." I said, "I am trying to follow more people so that I could keep up with what was going on in town." She said, "Hey, I'm having a get together at my place this afternoon. I do a little monthly thing for some of my friends who I am also connected with on social media." That day I got an invitation to go to a Happy Hour with a bunch of people who were Twitter users and social media users but they were not hanging out with the social media people. They were not the people who come to social media clubs and social media breakfasts and all these other things. They weren't tech people, at all. They were very light, casual users of this stuff. It was a totally different circle of people. I have already gotten one client and two perspective clients out of the people that I've met by going to that Happy Hour three times.

This kind of strategy absolutely can work if you are focused and thoughtful about who it is that you are adding and following. Like niche marketing, if you focus where it is and the kind of people you are adding it just gives you more opportunities.

Erik Wolf: *We are running out of time with you, but I have one more question on this very quickly. You did grow your base, really significantly in a very short period of time. I think it has only been a couple of weeks since I noticed that you posted that Tweet about increasing your follower base. Since then you have just blown* *up. How many man hours has it taken you to get from, you have increased about five times or more?*

Scott Allen: *I have gone from 4,300 followers to about 27,000-28,000 since April 1st or May 1st. In terms of man hours, that is the great thing, it actually only takes me an adding session, using the tools that I use, it takes me only 10-15 minutes of my time. I do that 3-4 times a week. Call it an hour a week, total.*

Erik Wolf: *Excellent.*

Scott Allen: *If you don't want to move as fast as I do, there are automated tools that you can actually set up and forget and they will add them for you. There is a really great one calledTwollow.com. What Twollow does is that you can put in a set of keywords and it will automatically follow people who are tweeting those keywords for you, every day. On the free account it will add about 10-20 people a day for you. If you pay a little premium, you can have it add a lot more for you. The idea, of course, is that you follow those people. You yourself should be tweeting about the things that you are looking for people to follow about. If they come back, if they are automatically following and they come back and look and they see that you are also tweeting about "green living" or "social entrepreneurship," or whatever it is, then odds are very good that they will turn around and follow you back.*

Erik Wolf: *It is part of maintaining the genuineness of what you are supposed to be doing out there as opposed to just blasting something out. It does keep it more real if you are targeting the people that you are going after.*

Scott Allen: *In general, in social media automating something that you would do by hand anyway, is not inauthentic.*

Erik Wolf: *The automatic direct message. That's something that people do because they don't really feel like direct messaging every single person that follows them.*

Scott Allen: *The Auto DMs, I am getting a lot of them. I did a breakdown of this and I would say that the numbers I ended up was about 80% of them are either out and out spam, or so blatantly self-promotional that they are just offensive, over 80%. About 15% are just kind of innocuous and don't really accomplish anything – "Thanks for following me, I look forward to getting to know you." If we just eliminated the 80% that are blatantly spam and self-promotional I don't think people would be nearly as offended by them. But, about 15% are just kind of innocuous and don't accomplish anything. About 5% actually either make me laugh, make me think, or make me want to contact the person or go to their website. In every case, it is brilliant copywriting. It is something out of the ordinary that really stands out, really brands them and is really engaging.*

If we could get it to where everyone was like that 5%, I don't think people would have nearly such a negative feeling of auto welcome messages. I had to turn mine off. I actually had significantly better response from people with mine when I had an Auto DM message. I had to turn mine off, though because there is a limit to how many DMs you can send a day.

Erik Wolf: *That's interesting…*

Scott Allen: *If I followed and then those people follow back and then I Auto DM them, I outrun my DM limit.*

Erik Wolf: *I wouldn't have actually known that. I have never run into my Direct Message quota.*

Scott Allen: *I was surprised too. I decided it was more important for me to do the mass following than for me to be able to have my Auto DMs. I did a split test. This is the thing, people can sit there and pontificate all they want. I did a split test of no message versus sending my Auto DM message. I found out that when I have an Auto DM message I actually only had one negative response from somebody, ever.*

Erik Wolf: *Really?*

Scott Allen: *Once that came up and I talked to some people, a couple of other people have said, "Yeah, I didn't really like getting the Auto DM." I actually only had one person out of thousands who actually said, "Don't Auto DM me. That's really offensive." But what I found was that when I didn't have an Auto DM that was engaging and authentic and the kind of thing that I would send somebody if I had time to do it all manually, I found out that the number of new followers who actually then engaged in conversation was actually 16 times higher than if I gave no response. 16 times higher that people actually came and started engaging me with either a DM back to me or app messages or re-Tweets or something like that.*

Erik Wolf: *Well, Scott, you've been breaking all the rules, all the things that people tell us not to do. We definitely appreciate your insight.*

Before we let you go, can we trouble you for some free advice for our listeners?

Scott Allen: *Absolutely. There are two things that go hand in hand, and they kind of go off of what I was just talking about. One is don't, I'm not going to say 'ignore the gurus' and I'm not going to say 'ignore the experts,' but I am going to say if you have a gut feeling or just what they are saying doesn't fit right with you then, by all means, feel free to try your own thing. But test it. That is the thing. It was the thing I did with my Auto DM. It was not that I just went the other way, I tested it and I showed that, yes the response rate is better, I have higher engagement with an Auto DM than not. My point is that you can break the rules, as long as you track what you are doing. If what you are doing is working then it doesn't matter if it breaks the rules.*

The other thing that kind of goes along with that is about social media engagement. One of the things I see is that I see a lot of social media experts talk about your social media engagement has to be steady. There needs to be some degree of steadiness. Obviously, you don't want to have something where you've created a blog and then there is not a post on it for three months. But, this idea that you have to be doing three posts a day to Twitter and five posts a week to your blog and that everything has to be a constant stream everywhere, is BS. Because, that is inauthentic. What is authentic is to publish when you have something to say.

The other thing is that the little hidden subconscious thing. Here is what happens when I don't post on Twitter for about a week. Then I don't post on Twitter for about a week, it is because I am working on something. It is because I am actually doing something. Social media silence doesn't mean that you dropped off the face of the Earth. It means you are actually doing some real work. When you come back from that, people are happy to see you. I get missed, people miss me when I am gone for a week, when I am not posting actively. I think the value of that is that there is a law of supply and demand. If people like what you have to say, then there is no harm in actually shortening the supply of it because then people are that much more interested and engaged when you come back. The thing is that you have been off and working and you then have something to talk about. Not only that, you reinforce that you do actually do work too and you are not just a virtual social butterfly out there on Twitter, Facebook and blogs all day long.

Don't feel the pressure, don't let people pressure you into feeling like you've got to keep this constant stream of output going on 17 different channels at once. It is absolutely okay to go off and get focused and get a big project done and come back and then talk about it. People will be happy to see you when you show back up.

Controversial Topic: How do I walk the line between personal and professional?

For many, especially those who have been in the business world for 20+ years, this is one of the scariest aspects of entering social media: that your clients, vendors, and business associates should have access to the same information about you online as your friends and family do. And the idea that your clients could be friending/following/linking with your employees is even scarier.

Here are four realities that we all need to accept in this new atmosphere of openness that social media and the Internet have conspired to create:

1. Any expectation we might have had previously about a clean "separation" of our personal and professional lives is gone. We used to be able to compartmentalize these things fairly easily, but social media has completely shattered that. Some would argue that it's made us all more whole and more human in a lot of ways as it allows you to add a lot of dimension to your relationships, but this is exactly what scares so many business owners. The people who connect with you online have the opportunity to learn a LOT about you and very quickly. Be prepared for that.

2. If you have employees, the online "bond" between them and your company exists as soon as someone self-identifies themselves as an employee online and many social media platforms encourage users to add their current and past employers to their profiles. Bottom line? This WILL happen. Expect that over time a large number of your employees, both present and past, will have your firm's name on their profile and expect that you will be permanently linked, even after that employee moves on.

3. Your company is going to have a presence on social media whether you want it to or not. The toothpaste is out of the tube so to speak and it's never going back in. Your only two choices are to A) participate or B) try to ignore it. If you're wondering, B is not a smart choice. Even if you aren't thrilled with the idea of trying to use social media in your business, at least participation gives you the opportunity to influence what is being said about you.

4. It's a good rule of thumb on the whole to just remove all your expectations of real privacy online. Never post anything ANYWHERE that you wouldn't want people to see. It's almost guaranteed that somehow, someday, that material will be discovered; maybe even by accident.

Hopefully we all understand that we're all in this social media thing whether we like it or not. So how can our businesses participate without the risk of embarrassing ourselves or being embarrassed by our employees? We can't. Unfortunately, the risk will always be there. But at the same time, the risk has also always been there that our companies might be embarrassed at meetings, sales calls, trade shows, networking events, via email, and over the phone. When these situations occur, we try to correct our errors as business owners and, in employer/employee relationships, managers use them as opportunities for coaching and professional development unless other disciplinary action is required. Social media is no different.

If you have employees, remember that their actions are ruled by self-interest. Ultimately, this is your only and most powerful defense against social media transgressions. It's in your employees' self-interest to behave appropriately online. The problem is that not many have taken the time to consider the larger implications of who they associate with on Twitter or what kinds of pictures they post on Facebook. Nobody has outlined expectations of professionalism or given them a friendly heads up that — if they aren't careful — their social media activities could cost them their job or help prevent them from getting another in the future.

For many of us, this is just common sense. But now there's a younger generation that grew up using MySpace and Facebook the way late Gen Xers grew up using email. We've got young professionals that have been managing profiles on sites like these since they entered college — or perhaps longer if they were early blogging adopters. These digital natives probably don't understand the traditional separation of personal and professional because they never experienced it. The best way, in our opinion, to ensure a seamless and relatively surprise-free entry into social media is to talk about it and try to prepare employees for it, just as you would prepare them for a big meeting or a trade show. And if things don't go as planned, a conversation needs to be had.

Social media is today what email was 15 years ago — a technology that's cutting edge (albeit overhyped), heavily consumed by young people and being adopted by businesses in greater numbers EVERY DAY. Your firm NEEDS to particpate or be left behind. Don't let any initial discomfort over crossing the "personal/professional" boundary be the excuse that keeps you on the sidelines.

Seven things we have learned from social media

We are not going to tell you that we know everything about social media and that hiring us will solve all your social media issues. Though we certainly don't discourage hiring us. But we are social media veterans — we really use the stuff and we have for a long time. Here's what the experience has taught us:

1. **We're HUGE on TWITTER:** Ok, not really. But using Twitter effectively has put us near the epicenter of the entrepreneurial "scene" here in Atlanta. But we have no illusions of becoming Internet celebrities anytime soon. As of this writing, however, both of us were ranked by Twitter Grader (twitter.grader.com) as being in the top 50... *thousand* Twitter junkies around. Don't try to be famous and don't worry too much about the number of followers you have or the number of times you update every day. People will be interested in you

because of the quality of what you say, not because you look important.

2. **Status updates aren't really about "what you're doing":** When you open up Twitter, the caption famously asks "What are you doing?" So without exception, every Twitter skeptic that we encounter in our travels asks "So why do people care what I'm doing right now?" They don't. And your Facebook friends and LinkedIn connections who may read your status updates on those sites don't really care either. They care about what you're INTERESTED in right now. They want to know what you've discovered today. What you're reading, what you might have learned in a conversation over lunch, what you're working on, what's making you laugh, the epiphanies that you have throughout the day. Sure, everyone posts mundane tidbits too, the "what are you doing?" stuff, but that's not what makes social media great. Focusing your status on something that has captured your attention makes you instantly relevant and gives you a unique opportunity to not only share but also contribute positively to someone else's day.

3. **Everyone has time:** Seriously. Twitter is only 140 characters at a time, a blog post doesn't need to be more than two paragraphs and it takes only seconds to follow up with new connections via LinkedIn. You can do this, really. Consider this: we make time to have coffee with

strangers that we meet at networking functions. Including drive time, you're probably looking at a two hour investment give or take. And that's just to exchange pleasantries with ONE person. Two hours spent on Twitter or LinkedIn can expose you to THOUSANDS of people. Now we didn't just say to abandon traditional networking. Don't do that. Networking with real, non-digital people is still very important. But you should view social media as a networking opportunity and give it the same attention you'd give an offline networking venue.

4. **You've got to give in order to receive:** Yes, much like traditional networking, you can't walk into a room full of people, shove a business card into every hand and then walk out expecting to get business even though you didn't stop to listen to what anyone else had to say. Likewise, you can't toss a handful of pithy remarks up on Twitter and expect to have 3,000 followers overnight. If you want people to follow you and read your updates, you need to read other people's stuff and provide feedback whether we're talking about Twitter, blogging, or any other media. It shouldn't be surprising that if you show an interest in someone else, they are more likely to show an interest in you. Yes, "digital" people are EXACTLY like their flesh-and-bone counterparts! The more you treat your online friends and associates like your offline ones, the better you will do. And be fair. Don't expect scores of followers or comments until you've accumulated enough content to pique their interest.

5. **Don't just do it at your desk:** Let social media into your world. Update your Facebook from a restaurant and tell us how the service is. Tweet on your way to a networking event (though not while actually driving, please) and let people know that you're going to be there. We've done that before and had several people actually searching us out before we got there (that will make you feel like a rock star, by the way). And that cell phone in your pocket is likely capable of taking photos and recording audio and possibly video. Create things on the fly and put them out there. It may be raw and it may take you out of your comfort zone, but it's unfiltered and genuine — everything that social media is supposed to be.

6. **Don't be a spammer:** Social media WILL drive traffic to your website. We have had months where over a third of our overall site traffic has come from social media sources. But don't force the issue. As Scott Allen says, only about one in every 20 updates should be shamelessly self-promotional. And when you are trying to get eyeballs on your blog and website, no need to be obvious about it. Post a link to your new blog post and tease us with the subject matter. "10 ways to save your professional sanity" with a link makes a much more enticing offer than "Read my new blog post."

7. **The real magic happens when you convert online relationships to offline relationships:** The next time you host an event, invite your local online connections. Attend a Tweetup (offline gathering of Twitter users) or a similar event. This happens to us constantly when we meet our online connections for the first time in person. People feel like they know you already, conversation comes easily and it is very easy to build a valuable relationship.

Overall, social media is a venue like any other where you tend to get back what you put in. Feed quality content into your social media ventures and you are likely to get good response and valuable new business contacts. What's the next step? Pick the tool that seems most comfortable for you and get started!

CONCLUSION

Hopefully by now you have a better understanding of what you need to do to kick your small business into overdrive. There's no one magic solution, of course. Each business is different so you have to decide what strategy works best for you and your company. The bottom line is this: You don't need a big company budget to look like one. Some of the things outlined in this book are things you can start doing right now. So make smart and unique choices about how to spend your marketing dollars. Where you spend your time will enable your company to grow more quickly than if you were simply trying to duplicate what worked for someone else.

Even if a larger competitor is doing something that may be working, don't think that this will work for your company. Besides, you'll pull your hair out just trying to keep up. Your company is unique even if you're competing with hundreds of others selling a similar product. Speaking of which, we're going to assume that you have a valuable product or service that people want because if you don't, no amount of great branding or marketing can make it sell. It might work initially but pretty soon, it will be obvious that you're selling snake oil. In the age of Twitter — where one person can blast out their satisfaction or dissatisfaction with your product to potentially thousands of people in a few seconds — make sure that you're being transparent, honest, and that you have a great product/service.

A lot of what we've outlined may require you, the entrepreneur or small business owner, to step outside of your comfort zone as well as your own perspective to make some of our recommendations work. Many entrepreneurs forget to see their company through the eyes of a prospective customer. This is a critical. If all of your branding, marketing, and public relations is highlighting what you think is valuable vs. what your prospects or customers think is valuable, then you won't do as well as you could. A great example of this is when Tropicana revamped its packaging and got an earful from their loyal consumers who had a deep attachment to the orange with the straw in it. In that instance, Tropicana wasn't looking at the packaging from their customer's point of view. They spent millions doing what they thought was best rather than what their customers liked. In the end, they went back to the original packaging.

Stepping outside of your comfort zone simply means that you have to be willing to try new things. A lot of business owners are hesitant to set up a blog because they're worried they won't have the time to contribute to it or that it won't necessarily help them gain new customers. But, a blog is virtually free to set up and can quickly establish your company as an expert in its industry and create a more personal relationship with your customers. That's just one example. If you commit to trying even one new thing per day (whether that's creating a blog, writing a white paper, calling a big prospect, or attending a networking event) then your business will grow. And, it will probably grow faster than you expected so be prepared for that.

A successful marketing and branding campaign can be both blessing and a curse. It's a good problem to have but you have to be ready when the orders start to roll in.

Getting featured on Oprah's O List is a huge win for a lot of companies but there are several examples of companies Oprah chose for her list that were woefully unprepared for what the publicity got them. Talk about a tremendous opportunity spoiled by lack of preparation. The publicity was still good but imagine if they'd been able to deliver. So, try to anticipate (if you can) what a windfall opportunity might mean for your small business. Before we leave you to your business and marketing planning, we've got one more tip to offer you:

Don't wait for perfection before you release your ideas, products, and marketing materials into the marketplace. Don't fall so in love with your ideas that you become incapable of ever letting them go. Our friend and colleague David Eckoff, an established technology entrepreneur and co-founder of the web startup Spitter, said it especially well, "Perfection is the enemy of innovation. Don't pursue perfection — first, it's expensive, unattainable and limits flexibility. Second, if your company waits to completely perfect a product before releasing it you'll never get anything out, you'll never ship anything. It's OK for your first release to be rough around the edges as long as it creates value where your customers need value."

Your marketing and your business don't need to be perfect. They just need to WORK. If your stuff doesn't ever make it to market, you'll never get the feedback you need to improve. Never stop tinkering. Never stop learning from the feedback you get along the way.

Oh, and good luck out there!

ABOUT THE AUTHORS

ERIK WOLF is a recovering corporate marketing director and the founder/president of Zero-G Creative, a marketing firm specializing in serving the unique needs of small businesses and startups. Erik also co-hosts a national weekly radio show called Gravity Free Radio where he has interviewed guests such as authors, marketers, bloggers, social media experts, entrepreneurs, sales strategists, and public relations professionals on subjects relevant to small business owners. **Follow Erik on Twitter at twitter.com/erikwolf.**

STEPHANIE FROST has worked in sales, marketing, and business development in a career that has spanned more than 15 years and a variety of industries. Stephanie is currently the Director of Business Solutions for Zero-G Creative where she works with clients to help execute marketing strategies that will meet their objectives without straining their budget. Stephanie is also co-host on Gravity Free Radio. **Follow Stephanie on Twitter at twitter.com/swfrost.**

**For more Information about
Zero-G Creative and Gravity Free Radio
visit zerogcreative.com + gravityfreeradio.com**

For information on some of
the subject matter experts
featured in this book and
a listing of helpful small
business resources
on the web, visit

marketingunmasked.com

Made in the USA
Charleston, SC
27 April 2011